Fostering Love

A Glimpse into Foster Care

Kathleen Paydo, RN

With foreword by Ron Paydo

Independently Published
WADSWORTH, OHIO

Kathleen M. Paydo, LLC
Wadsworth, Ohio, USA
KathleenPaydo.com

Cover Design: Lynde R. Kosko

FOSTERING LOVE

Kathleen Paydo – 1st edition

ISBN: 9780578377247

To our bios: Thanks for sharing EVERYTHING!

ACKNOWLEDGMENTS

My most sincere gratitude goes out to my parents for instilling a love of children in me, my mentors Tony and Diane Agnesi, for giving this project wings, and to two talented and endlessly patient ladies: Susan Ciancio, for her wise editing; and Lynde Kosko, for her beautiful cover design.

I would also like to express my gratitude to Ron, for always saying yes; to Matthew, for being my social media guru; to Elizabeth, for endless patience in helping me find my writing style; to Katherine, for kind emotional support; to Melissa, for running my "picking-up-the-pieces" personal hotline; and to Conner, who taught me how to turn on a computer that very first day.

CONTENTS

FOREWORD

Being a foster dad has been one of the most rewarding things I have done in my life. To fulfill this calling with Kathleen has been the best part of the journey.

Our goal has always been to make a difference and have a positive impact on those we meet. I often hear the comment, "I could never be a foster parent because I could never give the children up." While separation is very difficult, our job is to teach and guide the children during their time with us, not to keep them forever. The job of a foster parent is to act as a bridge for the children from the time they are brought into foster care until the time that an acceptable, safe, and permanent home solution is found.

Our family believes in volunteering and giving back as an important and vital part of our lives. Foster parenting has given us the opportunity to share our time, talents, and treasures with the most vulnerable among us. By nurturing these children in our home, we are hopeful they will impact society in a positive way.

Watching so many children heal and mature has been immensely rewarding, as we know we were there to protect them at a critical point in their lives. We then continue our efforts by guiding the children—one step at a time—to reach the goal of becoming a contributing member of society. I feel that we have also been able to significantly help many of the families of the foster children we have welcomed into our home. Understanding that we play a role in strengthening individuals and families makes the foster-care experience even more valuable.

I hope you will enjoy reading some of the experiences we have had with our foster children and the stories of how the children, in turn, have impacted our family. Foster care has been a phenomenal ride, and it's more fulfilling than I could have imagined when we began this journey almost thirty-five years ago.

There is no question that, done well, a good foster-care experience makes a profound difference in the children's lives. Take it away, Kathleen . . .

Ron

PREFACE

The journey through foster care is a fascinating one. The compassion I feel now for children manifested when I was just a child. My mother and father had taken me to see the play *Annie*, and I was profoundly disturbed by the way old Ms. Hannigan treated the little girls in her orphanage. I remember leaving the show and telling my father, "I'm going to have my own orphanage when I grow up so I can be nice to the little girls." To my surprise, when I was older, few orphanages remained in the US. After I got married, I was overjoyed that my husband, Ron, embraced the idea of becoming foster parents. We have opened our doors to foster children ever since.

Through the years, I started writing down foster-care "pearls of wisdom" as they came to mind. I tucked little pieces of paper away here and there so I would not forget what my foster children taught me or the funny things they said. As time passed, what became even clearer was realizing what a unique life we, as a family, were living. Many claim to know what living and working with different people from different backgrounds is like, but living the experience daily in your own home is truly something special. Numerous people have told me that I should write a book. After a lot of thought and prayers, I felt called to make known how special foster children and their life stories are.

Through many years of living with foster children, we have experienced hard days, rewarding days, and everything in between. We have had significant challenges, but we have also gained great knowledge, insight, and understanding. We acknowledge the pain—both physical and emotional—that our foster children have endured, but our beliefs center around allowing new beginnings to develop after previous bad endings. We focus on helping children heal, finding their momentum, and moving on to control their own destiny.

People tend to write off many of our country's foster children as problematic and nonproductive. True, some have significant problems they cannot or will not work to solve, but far more want to change the trajectory of their lives. In our home, I challenge foster children to rise above the temporary situation that is foster care and embrace having meaningful goals in life. I also dare our society to stand up and take notice that there is great potential for social change with these children.

Though the names of the children in this book are fictional, the stories are real, and I hope they will shed light on the truths and misconceptions surrounding the ever-changing world of the foster child as well as on the people in our communities who open their hearts and homes to them. There is a gold mine of promise wrapped up in the children who want to rise above their current circumstances. By fostering love, the potential exists to change our world for the better, one child at a time.

CHAPTER 1: FOSTER-CARE HISTORY

Interest in the foster-care world ranges from those who are simply curious about how the system works, to those who have a desire to become foster parents, to still others who have the power to provide positive changes in foster care. With each case, the circumstances and stories of the foster children change, but the joy of helping others only deepens. In one way or another, God calls many of us to this unique life.

Foster care has evolved significantly throughout the years. Long ago, large numbers of children who were found to be parentless and in need of care—especially in large cities such as New York and Boston—were "put out" on orphan trains and sent to the western states to be taken in by families to work on farms.[1] Some of the cases were presented to the public as positive, but most were still far from the expectations of modern-day foster care. Unfortunately, there are also terrible stories of children in foster care being "stolen" from their birth families and sold.[2] Many children were horribly mistreated, sold as slaves, and even murdered. Rarely did children get to stay together with their brothers and sisters. Modern foster care has learned tough lessons from history and seeks to correct the mistakes of the past while ultimately striving to give each child a safe and nurturing home.

While foster parents may be the primary caregivers, many additional people are needed to create a wider and stronger support system for foster children. I want to encourage a culture of excellence by first dispelling some of the myths surrounding foster care and then providing a clearer understanding of the amount of preparedness and ongoing support needed to thrive in this type of caregiving.

Historically, fifty percent of newly licensed foster parents quit after the first year of service.[3] For a higher success rate, foster parents need a realistic knowledge base, meaning actual tried-and-true parenting skills that will help offset the demands of the lifestyle. Many foster parents who leave foster care preface their resignations with statements of feeling forced to face challenges without appropriate support. Families exiting the system have explained that, once they accepted the child into their home, they felt like they were alone on an island. Ron and I have felt this way ourselves. There is a misconception that social workers or therapists will be present to help with difficult days as they occur. In truth, most days we are on our own as we problem-solve and navigate the children's behavior problems.

In our experience, the desire to help others and our strong spiritual strength are what help us weather most of the storms of foster care. We believe that God has called caring individuals, in many realms of life, to do whatever they can for the least of His children. He calls different people in different ways. In Matthew 25:40, Jesus instructs us, "Truly, I say to you, as you did it to one of the least of these My brethren, you did it to Me." This phrase, given to us directly by Jesus, has always been the inspiration for my family to provide loving foster care.

Our day-to-day strength comes from having an unwavering desire to help others, but we can only accomplish our goals by leaning on other foster families for support. The strong friendships with other fiercely dedicated foster-family friends are what make the job bearable. There are nearly 450,000 children across this nation who need foster care. The demand for excellent foster homes continues to increase, so building each other up in every way imaginable keeps us strong and determined. To help us remain quality members of the caregiving team, we must understand the history of foster caregiving coupled with today's modern needs.

Our first sibling placement was a brother and sister set named Amy and Jimmy. The agency asked if the children's mother could come and have her visits with her children in our home. We were new and trying to be cooperative, so we said yes. When the mother arrived, she asked if we wanted her to leave her gun in the car. We covered our shock and said, "Yes, please." While she never threatened us, she did later threaten another foster mom who had a third sibling in their foster home. After the uneventful visit, we contacted the worker on the after-hours response team to inform her about what had happened. She stated there was nothing more to be done and that she would file an incident report. This was our first unnerving occurrence of feeling unprepared for the vulnerability we would learn to face as a foster family, and it taught us early on that it is impossible to prepare ourselves for every scenario. We knew then that we had to find our own inner resolve and that being foster parents was going to require some bravery.

Our next placement call was just as much of an eye-opener. As we were sitting down to supper, the phone rang with a placement call for a seven-year-old girl, Coury. I was told by the social worker that she did not get along with her mother and that "the child had been thrown out of the house." She was coming into foster care with concerns of neglect. When Coury walked through our door, she was nonverbal, angry, and clenched her fists. Within minutes she threw a desk across the room, tore up her bedroom, and destroyed books. While we were shocked by this behavior, we knew the agency staff would not consider these mundane behavioral problems noteworthy. She had learned colorful language at home and used curse words to pepper every sentence. She had a dramatic and explosive personality and was eventually placed in a school that specializes in behavioral issues. Needless to say, being only one month into our foster-care career, we had to dig deep to muster the patience to parent her and to not be frightened away by these behaviors taking over our home.

Those who are intending to become involved with foster children should prepare themselves to make many sacrifices and be willing to put the needs of the foster children before their own. There will be comments from those who do not understand the true demands of the system, such as the familiar gut-wrenching statement, "Foster parents only do it for the money." Unfortunately, this is what some people think of foster-care efforts. While there are people in every field who do a miserable job in their area of expertise, most foster parents have magnanimous hearts and take children into their homes out of a desire to help them heal and grow.

By providing a clearer understanding of the amount of emotional and mental preparedness needed to care for foster children long term, I want to promote a high level of fostering that withstands the first year of licensing. My hope is that this book can provide real-world examples that make the current needs of both foster children and foster families better known to those in our communities. Our mission is to be mindful of the history of foster care, learn from the mistakes of the past, and support foster children today, in whichever way God calls us.

CHAPTER 2: TYPES OF FOSTER CARE

There are typically three types of foster care. Agencies differ on the terms and specifications of these, but they all entail having children in out-of-home substitute care. Some child welfare agencies offer a type of licensure called "foster only." Others offer "respite only," but by far the most common foster-care license is called "foster to adopt." We will examine all three.

Foster parents who solely want to provide "foster-only" care typically work closely with the foster child's family, as reunification of the child back to the family is the goal. The foster family actively supports the child's own family to meet the goals of the court-mandated case plan. This is basically the written plan of interventions the child's family must accomplish to get the child placed back with them. There is a cooperative back-and-forth working relationship between the two families. The foster home is not interested in adopting the child but will work tirelessly with the authorities to help find the best long-term solution for the child, even if they do not ultimately return home to their family.

Foster families who are interested in "foster-only" care should make their wishes known to the agency staff. If the situation the foster child came from seems to have a strong likelihood of reunifying, then the agency might attempt to place the child with foster parents whose focus is fostering only. This type of placement encourages the bonds with the child and their family to stay especially strong. Both families are working together to allow for consistent parenting techniques to be learned and shared with each other, which promotes a clearer understanding of expectations to the child. These interventions support stability within the family and a less chaotic environment. Once approved parenting techniques and disciplines have been successfully incorporated into the home of the foster child and a higher degree of safety has been established, the child is placed back with their family in reunification.

One child we fostered had a very dedicated and sincere mother. Nick ended up in foster care because his young mother was not experienced enough to know exactly how developmentally delayed he was. She knew that all was not well with Nick, but she did not understand all the aspects of care that her medically fragile child needed. She promised the courts she would work her case plan and commit herself to getting her child returned home, all while putting herself through school and working a job. She kept her word and did what she was asked. She gave up her vices, wholeheartedly participated in parenting classes, took additional medical training, and went to all the visits and most of the doctors' appointments for Nick. The mother was proactive with her communication to her social worker and worked hard to provide excellent care to her child. She participated with us weekly in "Help Me Grow" educational sessions in our home, along with Nick's therapist, to learn as much about his strengths and weaknesses as possible.

Gradually, the social worker arranged for extended visitation times, and Nick's mom had success with caring properly for her child on her own. Her case-plan objectives were met in a timely manner, and the courts sent the child home. Nick was very well bonded with his mother throughout the time he was in foster care. Happily, Nick (and his mom) still comes back to our home for occasional visits, and we continue to support this family in any way we can. What a blessing the foster-care placement was for Nick, the young mom, the attentive social worker, and for us—the foster family! In my opinion, this is the ideal way foster care is supposed to work.

"Respite-only" care is another type of foster care that some, but not all, agencies offer. This type of foster care is provided by a family that is a fully licensed foster home but that only provides temporary or respite care for a foster child who is already placed long term in another foster home. These homes are responsible for caring for the foster children at shorter intervals while giving the regular foster family a break. These placements can be for days or weeks and are a Godsend to full-time foster homes.

The ability to provide foster care year after year depends on these needed breaks, and these breaks can be a fun change in routine for the foster child as well. Ideally, the same respite home is used to provide consistent care for the entire time the foster child is in care. This consistency allows for the building of more layers of love for that child.

Lastly, there are blessed families who want to "foster to adopt." Foster-to-adopt families are willing to provide a forever home to a child who is not able to go back to the original environment from which they came. This situation usually occurs because of a failed case plan by the child's family or if there is no extended family or friends able or willing to take the child. Adoption is a true calling from God. These are beyond amazing people who succeed at raising children by providing a permanent environment for them to grow, thrive, and be loved!

One set of siblings—Whitney and Javon—were eventually adopted by the respite foster family we used. This family initially provided respite-only care but then completed the full program to obtain their license to become a foster-to-adopt family. Through multiple respite experiences with this family, a special bond formed. As Whitney and Javon's case dragged on, the likelihood of permanent custody seemed to be looming, as the children's family missed all visitation commitments for more than six months. The placing agency did finally allow for the children to be moved to this newly licensed foster home in anticipation of the courts awarding permanent custody of the children to the state. Eventually, the parental rights were severed by the courts, and these children were adopted by this family, with whom they were well bonded.

Some foster families are open to the possibility of an adoptive placement of a child from the start and let the agency staff know about this possibility should the situation arise. Others have a foster child in their home where the case plan evolves into a permanent custody case. This is when the legal status needed for adoption happens, and the family decides along the way to adopt the child. Being completely open and forthright with placement staff about intentions regarding adoption is a vital part of communication so that, when possible, children who may be at a higher risk of ending up in permanent custody may be placed with this foster-to-adopt type of home from the start.

Twenty years ago, a mother walked into our county agency and handed over her three young children. She told the staff she was not coming back, and they believed her based on the astonishing fact that she had done the same thing with her eight previous children in another state years before. These three children were immediately placed into a foster-to-adopt home. The courts and the assigned caseworker set up and offered a legitimate case plan to the mother, but they also started formulating an alternative plan of action to run simultaneously because of her history. This alternative plan would be a permanent adoptive home if the case plan were to fail. By strategically planning in this way, the likelihood of the young children getting to stay with one family throughout the whole foster and adoption process increased and created less disruption and better bonding for the children, which was what actually happened.

The primary goal of foster care is almost always to reunite the child with their family while keeping in mind that this realistically may not happen. State numbers vary, but in general about half of the children in foster care will go home to their family.[4] The goal of the agency staff and the foster family is to support the case plan that has been established for the child's family. Sadly, an adequate completion of the case plan does not always occur. The tricky part is that foster-to-adopt parents must, first and foremost, support the case plan and reunification of the child back to their family, all while being aware of the possibility of adoption as a backup plan.

There are times when foster families can be accused of sabotaging the efforts of a foster child's family to reunite with their children so that adoption with the foster family can occur. Cases and circumstances differ as widely as individuals do. Our own family has fallen victim to this accusation on occasion over the years, even though we have never once expressed a desire to adopt a child. We have had several families of foster children beg us to adopt their children; however, we do not feel that this is part of our personal calling. We want to continue taking in foster children without closing our foster home because of multiple adoptive placements. This is a very complex aspect of the foster-care world and is a challenge for even the most understanding agency staff and dedicated foster parents to work through.

For individuals pondering the world of foster care, the characteristics of these three types of foster care should be taken into consideration. It is important to understand each type of care because once you say "yes" to a placement of a child, that single case can last one or two years, or even a lifetime. Good or bad, each foster-care placement will make an impact on both families.

CHAPTER 3: A FOSTER CHILD'S POINT OF VIEW

With any type of learning, a person starts as an eager novice and learns lessons along the way. Our experience with foster care is no different. An important lesson we learned early on is that foster children have varying opinions and perceptions about foster care. One child will see the experience as a positive one, while another child may feel extremely negative toward the time in foster care. Foster children's mindsets are greatly influenced by their upbringing. They may even have preconceived ideas about foster care because, in the past, they were threatened by their family with being sent away to foster care if they were "bad." These children endure unimaginable hardships and are forced to witness abuses and neglect that can influence their point of view.

Recently, one set of teens, Miguel and Cheyenne, told us that their biological mom took them to the agency to drop them off and flat out told them she was never coming back. She was right; she never did. They told us they were glad for once that she kept her word and did not come back for them. As the months went by, it was clear that the abuse they suffered infiltrated every aspect of their lives and was so extensive that they considered themselves better off in foster care. Before learning about foster caregiving, I could never have imagined a situation such as theirs, and yet twice in our career we have witnessed this same sad scenario.

Indeed, the life of a foster child is difficult for many to truly imagine. We all have our preconceived notions based on either experience or on the horror stories we hear on the news. The need for a child to be placed in foster care usually starts with a dramatic and "final-straw" event involving their family. The police may break down a door to raid a drug house, the stolen car the child's family is riding in finally comes to a rest after a rollover, or the school principal has called the Children's Services Bureau (sometimes referred to as JFS—Job and Family Services—or PCSA, Public Children's Service Agency) for the seventh time that school year. Whatever the case, the family situation has climaxed. After that initial incident, everything in the child's life rapidly changes. None of the changes happening to the child or their family is comfortable, familiar, or solicited. (I typically refer to foster children's families as just that and not "parents" because so many children are being cared for out of home by extended family. Using the term "foster child's family" encompasses all these scenarios).

Though some foster children get a bad rap for being troublemakers, in truth, most are just vulnerable children who need stable homes, consistent rules, and caring, tenacious families. Foster children's problems range from common to supersized. Most have problems that stem from negative exposures in their environment and a lack of active parenting. Weighing in on how a child sees foster care is the fact that foster parents can be stereotyped as well. Some children are "briefed" on foster care by their families before being placed in a foster home, so they have preconceived notions before meeting us or fully understanding what foster care in our home is all about. Rarely are wonderful stories about foster parents told.

Regardless, no matter how problematic their home life is, most children do not want to go into foster care. This new world is filled with strangers and unfamiliarity. At the end of the day, their home and their mommy and daddy are beloved to them. A "social worker" is now in charge, and the children have little say about what is happening. Furthermore, there is an invisible "judge" somewhere making all the decisions. From a child's perspective, these people's jobs, as well as whatever a "case-plan objective that has to be met before they go home" is, are all completely foreign topics that need to be explained repeatedly by their foster family.

We received two little ones, Greg and Wendy, late one night after the car they were in never started up again after coming to a halt at a stop sign. The people in the car behind them noticed the driver slumped over the steering wheel. The dad was unconscious because of alcohol intoxication. They called the police who then notified Children's Services. The young children were still asleep in their car seats when they arrived at our house. The next morning, they woke up in a completely different home with a new mother and father who were trying

29

to guess what type of formula and pacifiers they would like. Change the drug of choice around and the aforementioned scenario has been the gist of the story behind several of our cases.

Losing familiar surroundings like their home is one thing, but children losing their parents and possibly their siblings is another. Two hours before the children came into foster care, life was normal as they knew it. Now, there is nothing normal about this new environment. From their point of view, almost everything is new: house, siblings, smells, dog, blankie, and pacifier. Alan, one young boy who came to us late at night, was distressed and confused because his little sisters were missing, and he did not know where they were. They had been taken into foster care earlier in the day. Alan's parents had told him to run and hide from the police officers, which he was successful in doing until he got scared and showed himself hours later. He was dazed by the time he made it to our house. Alan told us, "My dad is gonna whoop me cause he don't know where I am, and I lost my sisters!" He was horribly frightened. We reassured him again and again that his dad knew where he was and that his sisters had indeed been found, were safe, and he would be back together with them the next day. Still, he was highly anxious. No amount of explanation could quell his fear. In his mind, he was in a stranger's house, and his sisters were "lost," something he had been told to never let happen. The last thing he wanted was a new loving family when all he could focus on were these real-life concerns. Such big worries for one little boy of six.

Post-traumatic stress disorder symptoms are common amongst foster children. These highly stressful situations commonly create feelings of fear, anxiety, sadness, and hopelessness. Traumatic events, including those that brought the child into foster care, can cause delays in their thoughts, behaviors, and actions. While the child coming into foster care is likely experiencing feelings of confusion and loss, the foster parents are wanting to shower the child with affection. Realistically, most children have little idea what is going on and are not sure they are interested in being a foster child or having new loving parents.

Though many kind people will be caring for the children, it still does not change the fact that they have been uprooted from the familiarity of their families and that they are being asked to conform to an abundance of change. New foster parents, possibly new brothers and sisters, caseworkers, doctors, counselors, teachers, and classmates all want to be a part of the support system, but sometimes it is not what the children want. Foster children are forced to adjust. Continuing to inform them about what is happening to them and the exact nature of the role of all the new people in their lives will help ease their transition.

One element of care we like to explain to the children from the start is what we call "layers of love." We teach them that this is a special way to care for them and that it is meant to decrease their suffering and increase their comfort. Every service we successfully get in place provides support and strength to the child. This includes medical attention; proper nutrition; and a stable, happy home environment. The more layers of love we provide, the more we can help the foster child begin to heal and whittle away at layers of neglect and abuse. While it is impossible to solve all the children's needs during the time they are in our home, they will remember the genuine concern given them throughout their days or years in foster care.

A big part of being a foster parent is calming a child's fears in a way they can developmentally understand. We are sensitive to the fact that they are dealing with feelings of shock and are genuinely scared. An eight-year-old may have no idea what a judge or social worker is or even what foster care means. Just moments ago, home was home, and now they have gotten in a car and gone to live with a complete stranger. Many think, "This just isn't right. I've been told never to go with a stranger." When foster children are removed from their homes, a lot of information is dumped on them all at once. A foster parent speaks up and advocates to help the children feel heard by putting what is occurring into an understandable form. We want to positively influence the child's point of view about why they have been placed in foster care and help them transition into our care. As foster parents, Ron and I take the information overload and break the pieces down into manageable chunks that the children can comprehend.

Dispelling myths about foster care and giving emotional support to the children helps them begin to understand about the many people working hard to help their family succeed and reunify. We also want children to understand that they do not have to be forever defined by the traumatic events they have experienced. Trauma will always be a part of their history and touches their personality, but it does not have to be the final word. Foster care is presented to the child as a stage of their personal journey where trauma and victimization will be worked through, God-given gifts will be built upon, and finding their path will be the focus.

CHAPTER 4: LEVELS OF FOSTER CARE

Not all foster care is the same; different levels of need exist. The child may need a regular foster home or may need a home that specializes in increased behavioral and medical needs. Foster families come in all shapes and sizes. There are single- and double-parent homes with or without biological children present. Some foster parents are young, and some are retired. Foster families have different abilities as well. These factors all combine to determine which level of foster child is appropriate to be placed in which foster home.

Even though most foster homes are filled with charitable people, there will be critics who state that "foster parents are only in it for the money." I would like to ask them if they would work any job for twenty-four hours a day, seven days a week, 365 days a year for about a dollar an hour (before expenses). Truthfully, most foster parents dig deep emotionally and financially to provide for foster children. People taking time to learn about the world of foster care is an important initial step toward solving the current needs of foster families, no matter which form of interest or help you consider.

Typically, basic county foster-care programs are considered "regular" or "level 1" care. Children who are deemed level 1 should do well in a home-based environment with needs typical to other children of the same developmental age. Little Kyle and Josephine were typical eighteen-month and eight-month-old siblings. They ate finger foods, were working on drinking from sippy cups, and enjoyed gross motor play like riding scooters and swings. They were appropriately clingy and suffered from stranger anxiety when new case managers or other unfamiliar staff came to visit. They were typical developing toddlers and appropriate level 1 placements.

Children may have additional needs that are not always obvious at the time of placement. Since so many children come to us from drug- or alcohol-addicted parents, they suffer all kinds of unknown effects from their substance-exposed world. Sadly, because of rampant drug and alcohol misuse, almost all foster children in our society are negatively affected by these vices in one way or another. Impact from drug exposure can be direct, such as physical abuse, or indirect, such as the family's inability to make good decisions. Money allocated for rent or groceries might be used to buy drugs or alcohol, leaving their children lacking food. Even if they are not directly using themselves, older children can also be affected by substance abuse because they lack supervision and positive role modeling from their parents who are using.

People who have an interest in a more intense level of foster care might consider a private agency, as opposed to a county agency, because they provide higher levels of foster care: "therapeutic," "treatment," and "medically fragile." These types of foster care require additional training hours and experience because the foster parents take in children with emotional, physical, behavioral, and medical needs that are significantly higher than their peers. Definitions and parameters of higher levels of care differ with every agency. Suffice it to say, children who have more extreme needs than their peers would qualify for higher-level foster care.

There are also occasions when children are placed in a level 1 foster home when realistically they are not within the boundaries of what this level of care entails. Angel was a teen who needed therapeutic foster care. She was quick to throw objects at school when angry, disregarded her peers' and teachers' requests to respect their personal space, and was eventually expelled for safety reasons. She was impulsive in her actions, acting before giving much thought to consequences. She expressed great interest in fire starting, weapons, and ghoulish media. Angel required direct supervision most of the time because she was a danger to herself and others. After needing hospitalization, she was placed on a significant number of medications to give her better control over her mental health issues. Upon discharge, she was transitioned into a therapeutic-level foster home.

In all honesty, sometimes the acuity level assigned for the child at the beginning of the case depends more on which foster home had an open bed the day the child went into foster care rather than the realistic level of care the child will need, as was what happened in Angel's case.

Jamal (eight) and Lia (six) were siblings with extensive needs. Their personalities were extreme, and most days were filled with high emotion and drama. They were defiant about attending counseling and refused to participate on any level. They cursed at the caseworker and refused to give her requested information. We had a doctor's appointment where Lia would not let her blood pressure be measured, screaming at the top of her lungs to the nurse, "You're killing me!" Nor would she simply stand on the scale so her weight could be recorded. Jamal's teacher had to call us in for a conference regarding concerns of disrespect and stealing directly from the teacher's purse (repeatedly). Both kids were expelled from the bus the second week of classes for being physically aggressive with their peers. Jamal and Lia were diagnosed with developmental delays, emotional instability, defiance disorder, and interestingly enough, undiagnosed legal blindness. This all led to both children getting an individualized education plan (IEP) established and two times a week counseling sessions at school to correctly address their many needs.

One day while I was standing near Jamal, he quite unexpectedly turned and punched me in the stomach! What was so unusual was that we were having a nice conversation about his day. He did not appear to be upset or agitated but still hauled off and swung mid-sentence. When I asked him why he did that, he said he did not know why. I believed him because it came out of nowhere. A few weeks later, Lia was given a three-day suspension from kindergarten for frequently spitting at classmates. As these children were eventually transitioned to a pre-adoptive home (God bless that family), their behaviors were reevaluated and assessed to be appropriate for a treatment-level foster care. Unfortunately for us, we had been providing level 3 care most of the year with only level 1 support for each child. This was one of our most exhausting and difficult placements. Each child was charming in their own way, and we did have many fun days, but additional support was absolutely needed in the form of services and compensation.

Large sibling groups can also fall into a high-need category due to the difficulty of placing many children together in one home. One set of siblings we parented for a year had varying needs that ranged from medical neglect issues to academic delays, to mental health concerns, and to genetic abnormalities. Each child had special needs. Just the fact that we had five foster children in our home made the degree of care sky high.

Foster parents of medically fragile foster children are another specialized group that take advanced training focused on the specific medical needs of their current foster child. Medically fragile foster children can have global (all encompassing) delays for a variety of reasons, such as severe medical conditions, genetic syndromes, or physical abuse. Examples include children using oxygen with continuous monitoring, children with uncontrolled diabetes, or children on ventilators, to name a few. Medically fragile licensed foster homes are typically assigned social workers and staff who also have additional training to better understand the higher needs of the child.

We have provided every type of foster care at one point or another in our foster-care career. One medically fragile baby, Caleb, was born to parents who were hard-core drug users. He was born premature, heroin dependent, and later found to have genetic abnormalities. He also had immature lungs that affected the regulation of his breathing. Because of that, he used oxygen at all times and needed a pulse oximeter monitor attached to him every hour of the day to help us know that he was breathing effectively. In addition, Caleb was unable to swallow, so the doctors surgically placed a gastric tube from his stomach to the outside of his abdomen. This allowed us to hook up tube feeds that flowed directly into his stomach eight times a day. Wherever we went with him, we had a feeding pump, an oxygen tank, and a suction machine that accompanied us. Packing up little Caleb to take him out of the house was always an event.

During my pediatric rotation in nursing school, I was assigned the care of a toddler boy, Hunter, who had been born healthy. In a fit of rage, his father grabbed him by the ankles and swung him like a baseball bat, hitting his head repeatedly against a wall and causing severe head trauma and brain injury. Though he was alive, the once-healthy toddler was now in a permanent state of unconsciousness and would never walk, talk, or eat by mouth again. He was placed into a medically fragile foster home for long-term care once his condition was deemed stable enough to do so.

Learning the types of foster care and deciding between county foster care (typically level 1) or private foster care (typically therapeutic, treatment, and medically fragile care) helps guide a novice looking into the world of foster caregiving. The next step for interested individuals is to call the decided agency and sign up for pre-service training classes. Pre-service training is a series of instructional classes taken to begin learning what is needed to be a foster parent. The staff teach topics such as rules, regulations, stages of child development, parenting techniques, and how to fill out various forms should you become a foster parent. There are usually around ten to twelve classes that last two to three hours each.

After pre-service training classes are successfully completed, the prospective foster parents must fill out a packet of paperwork. This is a home-study packet and will contain forms such as a background check for each adult in the home, health history forms, driving records, financial disclosure forms, proof of insurances, completed CPR cards, veterinarian records (if there's a pet in the house), and more. Once the home-study paperwork is completed and sent back to the certifying agency, a walk-through home study, personal interviews, and a safety inspection of your home will be scheduled. Additionally, the home will have to pass various safety audits, including a fire inspection. Successful completion of the home study will result in the issuing of a foster-care license of the appropriate level.

Safety inspections of our foster home are done periodically by our agency staff (about every three to six months) to ensure that our home always remains in a state of good repair. On one inspection, my daughter's closet door was only partially open. The foster-care coordinator (the staff member assigned to our home at the time) asked me to fully open the other side of the closet because she had to make sure there was "no meth lab in it." I thought she was joking, but it turns out she was serious! They do look through every room and closet thoroughly. Only individuals who are serious about wanting to become a state-licensed foster home should start the home-study process because it is a great deal of work as well as a lengthy and expensive process for the county.

Since not all people will want to become licensed for full-time foster caregiving, some may choose to become an alternative caregiver for a foster family instead. Alternative caregivers are individuals who fill out minimal agency paperwork, pass a background check, and agree to the agency discipline policy. Alternative caregivers give rest to foster families and serve as a trustworthy person to provide a few hours of babysitting relief. Offering to be an alternative care provider for a foster family could be the ideal answer for people to help support the foster-care system without the heavy degree of commitment of becoming a full-time foster parent. This is a golden opportunity to educate others about foster care and how our society is truly attempting to improve the system by providing excellent care to these children 24/7 through good foster homes and fun alternative caregiver experiences.

Alternative caregivers are selfless people who help us take excellent care of our foster children, year after year, no matter which foster child is currently residing in our home. We always need and deeply appreciate the rest breaks. We have many relatives and friends who are approved respite caregivers who volunteer their services from time to time so we can take a day off. We consider these selfless interactions God's fingerprints, or small happenings, that occur out of the goodness of one's heart. We learned to recognize these gifts long ago and to graciously accept the help.

CHAPTER 5: THE FOSTER-CARE VOCATION

A desire to help others is why many people heed the call to fostering. Those interested in any aspect of foster caregiving may feel altruistic and want to help children by making them feel welcome and comfortable, while others want to fill a gap for the child by changing the circumstances of abuse and neglect facing them. Some people are dedicated to tackling a social challenge by fighting homelessness, trafficking, or addiction. Still others do not feel that they are quite done parenting yet. A mighty gift we have as humans is the opportunity to do good and choosing to act upon it.

All those years ago, basically as newlyweds, Ron and I started contemplating the idea of becoming foster parents. We began by educating ourselves about the various programs and needs in our area. This led to some interesting conversations with our extended families where we quickly discovered that asking the views of our family members and friends got us many differing opinions. We listened to their thoughts and concerns, sifted through the advice, and kept the ideas that we thought were helpful. We acknowledged that we would need to be cognizant of the amount of disruption to our own small childless family and by extension what our larger family should anticipate too.

We found there was some misunderstanding of the whole concept of foster care. Elders can mistakenly think that all the children will be kept forever, as they remember back to the times when foster children were basically taken in as workers for family farms. Shockingly, we were approached by an acquaintance who asked, "Why would you want to put your family through all of that?" Thankfully, there were far more gracious relatives and friends who went above and beyond to support us every step of the way.

We pressed on and considered the characteristics of children we thought we would best be suited to help. We attended pre-service foster parenting classes, which gave us a cursory-level understanding of what fostering was about. We then went through the home-study process and got our foster-care license over the next year. We were surprised what a huge learning curve there was from what is taught in class to what is learned along the way. What was most important, though, was knowing we wanted to change the course of children's lives by giving them a stable home. As a top priority, we always kept in mind the idea of strengthening our own family unit by adding the foster vocation to it. Ron and I agreed long ago that when the foster-care experience started taking away from our own family strength we would stop. We have not reached that day.

In the first few years of our foster-care career, before Ron and I had our own children, we fostered one or two children of any age at a time. We became more proficient in learning the ins and outs of the system after parenting our first twenty foster children, who ranged in age from newborn to seventeen. Eventually though, we paused our foster-care career and took a long break to spend time solely raising our four young biological children. One day, during the end of this ten-year break, as we walked out of church, I told Ron that I felt God calling us back to the foster-care vocation. He chuckled and said, "Well, He may be calling you, but He's not calling me." That lasted only a few minutes before we were both in agreement that we had more parenting love to share with God's needy children, and we started the process to get a foster-care license for the second time.

As we returned to the fostering vocation, we decided to take in foster children who were the opposite ages of our children. The driving thought was that not all the children would need the same amount of attention at the same time of the day. For instance, when our biological children were young, we took in mostly teenagers. We knew we would likely have our children's busy bedtime routine earlier in the evening, leaving later hours open to tend to preteen and teenage children's needs. We also had time to allow participation in sports, as our biological children were not yet old enough to play in organized leagues. This worked out very well. Eventually, as our children aged, we fostered younger children, knowing we were already busy with sports, youth groups, and Scouts, and we did not wish to add more busyness to our schedule with additional school-aged needs. Packing up strollers full of little ones to take to older children's activities worked out well at that point in our lives.

Somewhere along the line, our vocation niche began to focus on wanting to keep siblings together. Ron and I always felt strongly that if a situation ever warranted our four children to be removed from our care, we would absolutely and without a doubt have wanted them all kept together. When surveyed as adults, foster-care alumni put losing their biological siblings as by far the most important bond they felt should have been upheld while they were in foster care. They consistently rank the sibling bond even higher than wanting to be reunified with their parents.[5] As we became increasingly comfortable taking multiple children into our home, we decided to make the desire to primarily take sibling groups known to our agency staff.

Since then, our family has had the pleasure of fostering many sibling groups. Typically, three to six children are common. One summer afternoon though, we were called about a sibling group of eight, all under age eight! While it was not our plan to take in eight children, after consideration we thought that, with enough help, we could manage—all in the hopes of keeping the large sibling group together. As the terrible details about this home situation were revealed, we felt confident in our decision to extend ourselves farther than usual. Ron contacted a local car dealership to see if they could get us a larger vehicle, and our teenage children and I started arranging bedrooms and clothes. We began to work through countless other details pertaining to how we could realistically manage these children. After forty-eight hours of preparation, the day arrived for the mother's scheduled incarceration to begin. However, at the last moment, a grandmother was approved to take the children into a kinship placement, so they never ended up at our home. Still, in the end, we were ready to attempt this large sibling placement, even though it was out of our usual comfort zone.

Years of experience of fostering in varying situations have matured us as foster parents. Fostering children successfully has little to do with what you learn in books and manuals but rather comes from WANTING to understand why children act the way they do. Non-traumatized children bring their own challenges, but not to the degree of a traumatized child. The way foster children think through and process a situation is often so obscure that it can be difficult to understand their thinking or anticipate their responses. We use controlled trial and error and adjust our techniques for each child based on what we see the child's reasoning is and why they chose the action they did.

Tackling social change has become increasingly more important to us through the years. Ron and I speak to many able-bodied families of our foster children and help them understand that they do have the ability, as well as the responsibility, to make choices to alter their life's trajectory. We try hard to be empathetic to their stresses and are supportive of them using appropriate public services as a short-term solution, but this is not the end of our support. We keep in contact with, and in many ways advocate for, our old families. Misconceptions exist that people cannot work their way out of their problems. We know this is not true for most.

In addition, we develop a strong protective tendency toward the families of our foster children, always promoting the fact that they are beloved children of God who are capable of change and that change is good. These families need others to cheer on their efforts to parent effectively and take control of their lives. Coaching the family members along is a big part of our mission. As the adults stabilize, we encourage them to focus on their talents through education and steady employment as a means of surviving long term and to be an excellent example to their children. To date, all of our former foster children (the ones who are now adults) whom we keep in steady contact with are gainfully employed and successfully raising their own children.

We want leaders in our communities to know that young families tell us how much they want to break the lifestyle of being dependent on others. They express that being constantly dependent on others' support makes them feel that they are incapable, downtrodden, and trapped. Most want a better way of life for their children than what they are currently going through themselves. They vehemently wish for their children to stay away from the drug scene. We tirelessly support their efforts to move their lives in a positive direction.

One important form of support is being a role model. Ron hails from corporate America as his "other" vocation. This world is filled with hardworking people whose work ethic allows them to accomplish a great deal. This is not by happenstance. These people accomplish successes through endless hours of hard work, sacrifice, and determination. Ron uses his analytical skills to evaluate all aspects of a problem before deciding on a plan of action, and he has taught our family to do the same. He encourages working through problems by using creative thinking, listening to others' ideas, learning from mistakes and repeated adjustments, and evolving the problem into a workable solution. Children must learn that others cannot solve all their problems for them. Just because problems do not come with a manual does not mean children are incapable of figuring out a solution. Teaching our children how to identify their abilities and demonstrating the process of how to use those abilities helps us improve our society one child at a time.

Ron and I encourage our children to think critically. We feel that the best way to get past a problem and to reduce stress levels is by finding a suitable compromise and avoiding endless conflict. Chronic stress is not healthy for children. Years ago, we had four sisters who struggled with their highly disappointing relationship with their mom. She had let them down by failing to provide stable housing—including heat or running water—and with her inability to protect them from chronic hunger. Furthermore, she turned a blind eye to relatives who abused them physically and sexually. One sister felt sorry for her through it all. One stood up for her at all costs. One did not ever want to talk about her, and one was constantly angry with her. Through many months of counseling, the sisters all had to find a way to come to terms with the feelings associated with their mother's profound neglect. One sister wrote songs about her feelings, the next worked on being the less parentified child in the family and tried to regain her childhood, the third worked on maturing herself up enough to forgive her mom, and the fourth learned stress-relieving techniques (she chose to shoot endless baskets with her pink and purple basketball) to curb her angry outbursts.

These girls learned the value in finding interventions that they felt were useful in helping move themselves from victimization into forgiveness and recovery for the bad parts of their upbringing. We talked to them about choosing to focus on the goodness of their everyday lives. In other words, their mother's lack of protection was a terrible injustice, but they individually got to be in control of determining if that suffering would define them forever or not. Discerning what they wanted to do with the rest of their God-given, able-bodied lives was highly encouraged, but it was ultimately for them to decide. Thankfully, they all seemed to be edging toward that goal when the call for them to go home was received. This is an example of how we are sometimes left with only fervent prayers that our seeds of recovery, hope, and grace will continue to grow in these children.

As we enter the next stage of our lives, Ron and I want to promote foster care on a larger scale. This includes conversations with agencies, corporations, and governments in the hopes of educating others in ways to improve the day-to-day needs of foster children. Much of this includes encouraging professionals to share their talents and leadership traits, which can dramatically impact foster youth. Simply spending an hour in a new environment participating in an activity that the child previously has no experience with can make a lasting impression.

Recently, during a snow day off from school, Ron took our eleven-year-old foster son Buck to a meeting with the mayor. He then got to tour City Hall and see a brief government meeting. He was given a photo of himself meeting the mayor, which he decided to share with his class the next day at school. Buck reported back to Ron how "cool" that experience was for him and that several students approached him on the playground and wanted to hear more about the day he spent at City Hall with his foster dad. Youngsters need these experiences to give them an understanding of the bigger world around them. Children blossom when work ethic and proper social skills are explained, demonstrated, and taught. Ron and I think piquing a child's interests by having an opportunity to experience something novel, like a meeting with a local official, is the reason children's behaviors settle down and grades improve so much when they are in foster care.

Our goal is to support the fostering vocation by promoting changes that lessen hardships on the foster family and that lead to better longevity of service. All these factors will, in turn, improve the life of our country's many foster children. Further, we want to increase government officials' awareness of the reasons for the tremendously high turnover rate of despondent foster parents and explain how this affects their county budgets. Successful fostering centers around healing the child, meeting them where they are developmentally, teaching about choices, and watching them grow past their difficulties and into a state of adjustment, all while cheering hard along the way.

My family's reasons for wanting to foster have evolved over the years, and our story looks different from any other family's story. Initially, we had to put my nightmares of Ms. Hannigan in the story of *Annie* to rest. Later, we felt drawn to the Bible verse Matthew 25:40 and the desire to care for children in need. As time went by, we realized that our years of experience and deep understanding of the plight of foster children led to the desire to pass information on to others. Currently, we feel a fiscal responsibility toward various levels of government to help them understand how foster parents can realistically withstand the system long term and what effects this will have on their foster children and budgets.

However, these efforts always center around wanting our foster children to be incredibly proud of who they are and to know that they are capable and highly valued individuals. We plant many seeds of encouragement, hoping this unconditional love will eventually have a positive impact on our foster children and their families. By showering children with the greatest amount of love and support we can, we hope to see positive change reflected in our communities.

CHAPTER 6: THE BIOS

Biological children raised in a foster home are simply amazing individuals! There is not nearly enough attention given to the sacrifices of this unique group of people. Strong family bonds are what enable families to endure the challenges of having foster children placed in their home. Ron and I would not consider being foster parents without the support of our biological children (affectionately referred to as the bios). We acknowledge that our biological children lived through many days that were out of their control and sacrificed much throughout the years. Foster children's needs must be woven into the fabric of our family's life, not the other way around where our family identity is lost in the process. We always felt a strong calling to be foster parents, but that calling never came before the needs of the bios.

Our own children came along through the first ten years we were foster parenting. With the birth of our fourth child,

Matthew, we took ten years off to concentrate solely on raising our biological children. Years later, when Matthew was ten, we restarted the foster-care licensing process. At this time, our children ranged in age from ten to sixteen years old. We felt they were old enough to ask their opinion about fostering. (In full disclosure, apparently when they said yes, they didn't know they were agreeing to an unending time frame). Still, when everyone agreed, we worked on preparing for the upcoming lifestyle change.

As a family, we discussed the type of child who would fit best with our family dynamic. We worked together to identify a desired foster-child profile that would help to increase the chances for a positive experience for the foster child, and we paid attention to the suggestions of the bios as to whom they thought they would enjoy having as a sibling. This communication was important to us, as we knew this would be a massive family undertaking. As our children aged, we adjusted the ages and group size of foster children to fit our family best at that time in our lives.

Biological children growing up in their parents' foster home need to be taught to understand the foster-care system as their age and development warrant. We all assume that everyone knows what foster care is, but not all children do. We once had a ten-year-old foster child who, after several weeks in our home, asked, "Who's a foster child?" As a result, we make it clear what the whole foster-care process means to each child in our home. We explain that we are helper parents who work with police officers, social workers, nurses, and doctors and that we take in children whose families need extra help for a while. Further, we emphasize to foster children that we are going to take excellent care of them until their mommy or daddy can do so themselves.

Through continuing-education training, we kept our children in the loop about pertinent information we were learning so they too were as prepared as possible for having siblings with different needs. We went into the second phase of our foster parenting vocation with more of a team effort attitude. Typically, the bios were older than the foster children and could be more helpful in caring for them. Our biological children turned out to be very helpful in standing together to show a united front in obeying us and following rules, setting a good example for the foster children in our home.

A foster family we knew took a different—and detrimental— approach to explaining foster care. They expressed to their only child that they felt like someone was missing from their family and that they were choosing to pursue foster caregiving as a result. I believe the parents were well intentioned with wanting siblings for their only child; however, their plan backfired because their biological child became increasingly depressed and was very much a recluse as she made her way through her preteen and teen years. The foster parents disclosed that once, during a counseling session with their now-adult daughter, she said that she had always felt like she let them down, which led them to want to foster. In my opinion, to be most effective at foster parenting, parents must keep biological children the priority of the family.

Before a new child comes into our home, I usually inform my husband first. I say *usually* because, depending on time and circumstance, sometimes he just walks into a surprise. Next, we inform our children of any upcoming changes in family members and explain that their job is to be accepting, kind, and supportive to all the new children. It is important to explain the expectation with biological children that foster children's information is private and cannot be shared with friends. We would remind our children that foster children's faces could not be shown in photos on social media and names could never be revealed. We taught them to instead use terms such as "little one," "fella," "kiddo," or "pal" to not compromise privacy or safety.

Changes in birth order can be a huge challenge that biological children face. Very young biological children will likely look at other young foster children as playmates with the usual jealousies and arguments that would occur among any group of youngsters. We used caution when we took in foster children who were older than our biological children, always wanting to be sensitive to their leadership role and birth order in our family. Keeping biological children's feelings and needs in mind with each placement call is vital. We all want to be sure that we are not taking away from our own children's love and affection but are instead mustering up extra for the foster children.

One way to respect biological children is to be watchful of which children will be asked to share a bedroom. Most of the time we allowed our bios to share their bedrooms with each other only. On occasion, an extra bed was added for a foster child, but only with their permission. State rules require that all children in a bedroom must be under the age of five if both girls and boys are sleeping in the room.[6]

The effects that foster children have toward the biological children in the family must be given serious consideration. Many years ago, we had a foster teen who smoked. This information was either not known or not disclosed to us when we accepted her into our home. Her own mother provided her with cigarettes at every weekly parental visit, which used to be allowed. Our newborn infant, Elizabeth, developed respiratory syncytial virus and asthma, which our pediatrician said were likely a result of secondhand smoke exposure, even though the smoking occurred outside. We were crushed. We learned the hard way about RSV dangers with infants and smokers. At times, we must prioritize and choose our own family's needs first and say no to a foster placement altogether.

We have always worked hard to keep our children educated regarding their own safety around foster children and their families. Ever since they were young, we enforced strict boundaries. Our children knew to have two family members together in a room when a foster child with particularly high risks was present. Changing clothes, bathing, and personal time were all provided in private spaces for both our biological children and foster children. They were instructed to say "NO" loudly and clearly the minute any infringement of their privacy occurred. We ask all children to be open and bring any concerns they have to our attention immediately.

From time to time, we review appropriate and inappropriate touch with all family members. No tickling or roughhousing is permitted in our home because innocent fun can be interpreted as not-so-innocent. Children might be too naive and affectionate to know that lap sitting could be misinterpreted by a foster child or trigger the memory of a traumatic event for them. As a general safety rule, we teach that lap sitting is not permitted. Babies, of course, are an exception.

We practice glove wearing and avoid touching body fluids (because as a nurse, this is a hard habit to break), as we know realistically that anyone can have hepatitis, HIV/AIDS, or many other infections. For example, twelve months after a child had already been in their home, one family found out that their foster child had been born from a mother who had AIDS. When they found out, the child was then scheduled to be tested, but until that time and for the whole year previous, they were not aware of the increased potential risk. The agency staff cited that the information was confidential. I never quite agreed with that stance in this situation, but there are so many unknowns with the foster children's history that we want to err on the side of caution using universal precautions with every child.

One sweet benefit of having foster children in our home is that the unique experience affects more than just our own biological children. For instance, friends of our children showered the foster children with extra affection when they were at our home. Melissa, Katherine, and Elizabeth—our daughters—had high school girl friends who would offer their talents in giving us help with little-girl hairstyles, and Matthew's friends would gather up little ones and give them piggyback rides across the football field. We had many helpers at the sports events we attended with little children in tow.

Many of the teens did not have experience with younger siblings, so they enjoyed getting to know and play with the children. Of course, the fosters thrived with the added attention too!

Biological children see how hard their parents work doing their part with the child welfare system. They see their parents frequently on the run with appointments. On occasion, they hear unkind comments about the characteristics of their family. They witness the damage that happens to their home and at times to their own personal items. They learn to live with less calm time in their lives and endure stresses associated with constantly changing schedules and differing members of the family. They know they will bond with some foster siblings better than others and that many goodbyes are hard.

One little six-year-old boy, Chris, did not mesh well with our family. Chris was aggressive, defiant, and violent, and his destructive behaviors upset the bios. There were many stressful days and sleepless nights with Chris and his siblings in our home. When their foster family from years previous contacted the agency and expressed a desire to foster-to-adopt them, we readily agreed to the transfer. We came across a saying shortly after these siblings left that says, "All our visitors bring us happiness, some by coming and others by going." Goodness, some days, it is true.

It's fun to go back through our list of foster children and reminisce which foster child bonded with which biological child. Melissa enjoyed Aisha's sassy antics and liked being able to reconnect with Noah and Bruce as adults. In fact, they went to each other's weddings. Katherine thought sweet little Rose was the belle of the ball because they both shared a love of princesses. Katherine, who aspired to be a teacher from a young age, was especially empathetic to the little ones who struggled with their school lessons. Elizabeth was partial to Jana's sweet special needs and George's toothy smile. Kyle and Josephine were also near and dear to her because they survived a kidnapping. Matthew shared his love of rap music with Jeremiah and Howard, felt connected to twin tots who had matching miniature eyeglasses that looked like his, and lastly thought Tre and Gabby were wonderful because he liked their kind personalities.

As our children started to head off to college, we shared some additional safety tips about foster care. Ron and I instructed them to never engage in a power struggle with a family member of a foster sibling if they happened to run into one in public or should an abduction look like it was occurring. Our children know to not intervene. They are to state clearly and calmly that the authorities will be notified. Running into family members in public has happened to us several times. We let the children visit for a few minutes then head on our way. We have never encountered any problems. In fact, Matthew ran into Nick and his mom one day at the store and said they all hugged, visited, and took pictures like a bunch of old friends.

Over the years, our biological children developed a strong sense of caregiving as they helped care for the various foster children placed in our home. Now, as young adults, they have a wide variety of experiences to draw from. Matthew has been my saving grace on more than one occasion when he tends to a foster child at his college for an hour or two while I head down the road to a court hearing for a foster child. He says he gets some interesting stares while pushing a stroller around campus, but at pickup time it is clear that his hovering friends, who are busy taking turns pushing the stroller, have really taken to the children. I have been heard referring to Elizabeth as my "right hand man" because there are days that she runs my home better than I do.

Our biological children received an early education on substance abuse and its effects on the family. They know about human trafficking and prostitution because some of the babies we get are a result of that lifestyle. They know the signs and symptoms of abuse, neglect, and domestic violence, and they know how to use non-judgmental kindness to soothe the feelings of little ones. They know about redirecting children away from negative behaviors and how to "hurdle help," or assist, one who is struggling. They know how to manipulate the environment instead of getting into a power struggle with a child. They readily tutor all grades. Katherine, who is now a teacher, has been immensely helpful in instructing me how to identify correct reading levels, educating me on the rationale for using number lines for addition and subtraction instead of counting on fingers, and guiding me when to request a formal school assessment.

Biological children who grow up in a foster home understand developmental delays, handicaps, signs and symptoms of various illnesses, and gross and fine motor skill levels. They all know (as well as any friends who are over for the day) how to properly install car seats and can assemble and disassemble beds in no time flat. They know CPR, first aid, proper oxygen levels, and how to suction and do a g-tube feed. They understand that concentration, organization, time management, and follow-through are skills that must be mastered, especially in a busy, energy-filled home environment. They know true compassion and empathy for others. I do not write all this to boast about our children but to communicate the wonderful blessing foster children can bring to a home and to show how much we have all learned from the program.

For three decades, we have affirmed to our children how much we appreciate their willingness to participate in the foster-care life. They understood that as they aged, grew more independent, and earned new privileges they should continue to include our foster children whenever they could. They have all been through Scouts and know how important it is to be an inclusive leader, to spend quality time with the children, and to be a good role model. One set of siblings was enamored with the fact that Melissa was a real scientist. She is also the master at teaching, with unending patience, the rules and strategies of games. Six little girls and one pack of Old Maid cards make for some hysterical game sessions. Her husband saves me the time of getting wheelchairs and bicycles adjusted because he can fix anything he sets his mind to. We stress that we are all helping carry out God's work, and they have been good stewards to this calling.

Experiences such as these help us keep our focus on a life of service. Over the years, when asked, our biological children generally felt connected to our foster children as long as they did not have huge behavioral problems or were excessively disruptive to the family. They also take pride in our life's work. Ron and I feel that when our children witness us being "others centered" they will follow in our footsteps to some degree and will find their own volunteer niche that suits their lives.

I shared a cute story of a foster boy named Andrew with my adult children one day. He arrived late at night sound asleep in the back of a police squad car and barely even remembered the officer carrying him into our house. The next morning when he awoke, he saw a small area of green grass outside and could not believe that was our grass. As a boy from the city, he was amazed that we were actually allowed to walk on it. I still remember the joy and energy in his leaps and bounds when I asked him if he would like to run across the grass and roll down the hill, which I literally had to demonstrate. I will never forget the image of his authentic happiness. To this day, every time I look at that grassy knoll I am reminded of the gift of open land, Andrew's happy laugh, and the joy foster children bring to our family.

We have always encouraged close bonds between our biological children because they can be a strong support for one another and help catch what Ron or I might be missing because, honestly, we have all faced many foster-care challenges together. One keen-eyed biological child may notice discouraging feelings of a sibling before a parent does. We take the time to remind our family of our strengths and blessings when we can see the family dynamic is off, but on days that our bios are overwhelmed with their own needs, we take a step back and ask an alternative caregiver for a few hours off to spend extra time with them.

The absolute best way to stay connected to our children has always been through Sunday morning Mass together. While it is no longer possible to always be together in person, we do love the Sundays that our adult children are all in town and we get to attend Mass as a family and then share a meal together. We also get that needed family support by attending Matthew's weekly Catholic Youth Organization volunteer commitments, sharing in Elizabeth's love of her Newman Center work, participating in Katherine's Catholic school's first grade class student fun days, and watching Melissa and Conner through online Mass participate in parts of the Mass as Eucharistic ministers and lectors from several states away.

Beyond that, our family stays close by being informed with daily briefings with each other. These conversations are a great way for each member to take turns reporting on their day's events and to stay in touch with each other. We used to laugh at young Matthew, who would start off his allotted time with, "Well, first I got up..." We knew to get comfortable because a dissertation of his day was coming. With all of today's technology choices, we still easily talk to our adult children daily. Melissa calls at lunch, Katherine calls after work, Elizabeth calls midafternoon, and Matthew calls after supper. We may only chat for a few minutes, but it gives us time to reconnect, and it is a chance for Ron and me to tell each one how grateful we are that God gave them to us. These fun bantering sessions keep us on the same wavelength with each other and allow for some good laughs. Through cheerful and encouraging conversations, we want to make it clear to our bios how important they and the events of their lives are to us.

Keeping our bio children front and center of our parenting dreams meant additional projects from time to time. For example, we ended up adapting the foster child Lifebook idea (explained later in this book) for our biological children too. I decided that while I was committed to making memory books for our foster children, I desired to document the important events in our children's lives as well. I wanted to show our children that their hard work at church, school, volunteering, and extracurricular activities was important enough for me to take the time to document. It was a big-time commitment, but I enjoyed doing it for them. I cannot think of a more effective way to boost any child's self-esteem than to highlight the accomplishments of their life. Biological children need this support just as much as foster children.

Biological children raised in the foster home setting face a unique upbringing—an upbringing that is not always easy—and they will sacrifice a portion of their parents' time and attention along the way. They deserve to feel cherished and to receive our most devoted love. On occasion when one of the bios feels that they are being shorted, they will sarcastically yell, "Call my worker," wishing they had someone official to listen to their woes. But all joking aside, we often thank them for living in a home with an atmosphere of purposeful busyness and one that requires extra work from them. We are grateful for the fact that it was effortless to raise our bios to love others unconditionally in the ever-changing and unique environment that we call home.

Foster children are very important in our lives, but having an intact, close-knit relationship with our biological children always remains our primary goal. Without a stable family of our own, we would be less helpful to the needs of the foster children and their families. The best we can do to support our family is to understand that we could dread every situation associated with foster care or instead choose to keep the tough days in perspective. Ron and I help our children concentrate on the positive aspects of being a sister or brother to a foster child and encourage them to not focus excessively on the negative points. We have all had the opportunity to help the children of the foster-care system and have witnessed tenfold the blessings brought to us.

CHAPTER 7: RELATIONSHIPS

The single best part of foster caregiving is the relationships that form along the way. There are amazing connections with foster children of course, which often by extension include the children's family members. Developing bonds with peer foster-family friends, school staff members, agency personnel, and authorities of the courts are also highly worthwhile. Since foster care is a life mission, our stamina and general outlook on life are better when we surround ourselves with great people to share the foster-care experience.

Our relationship with our many foster children spans from sweet babies and toddlers to now adults. Many children come into foster care downtrodden and hopeless, and our work is to do what we can to correct that. It is difficult to put into words the mama and papa bear fierce protective feelings that start the minute we lay eyes on our foster children. We have, after all, experienced a true sense of appreciation from the children for being properly cared for. Even small children seem to understand thriving on the proper care and affection given to them. Meeting the needs of the child is what makes deep bonds form between foster children and foster parents.

Tre and Gabby continue to come back and visit us years after being adopted. Our relationship is longstanding, thanks to their generous adoptive mother who is kind enough to allow us to continue to be occasional alternative caregivers for the children. They have grown into the sweetest children, which is such a tribute to their adoptive mom and grandfather. We often point out to the children that they are lucky to have so many people who love them. They have the family they were born into who cannot take care of them, but who still loves them. They also have a foster family to spoil them just a bit on special weekends, and they have a dedicated adoptive family who is lovingly committed to their ongoing happiness and strong formation.

One of my favorite bonding rituals that Ron has developed with all our foster children begins when he walks in the door from work and starts this funny formal exchange of greetings with them. The small children run over to line up to take their turn talking with "Mr. Ron." He has these sweet miniature "business meetings" with each child. They dramatically shake hands and are greeted with a booming, "How do you do? My name is Daddy!" Yes, babies included. The toddlers will answer back, "How do you do? My name is Reanne"—if they can get through all the laughs and giggles. He also greets every older child by name with a warm hello. Typically, Ron then takes all the children, young and old, outside to shoot baskets or to toss the football around to give me time to finish the meal preparations and clear my head. If the weather is too cold outside, they use our indoor basketball hoop in the basement play area. Over dinner, he asks each child, no matter how old they are, how their day was and listens intently to their responses. He has a great way of using his upbeat antics to connect with the children.

Fathers are certainly a missing piece in the lives of many children we foster. One young fella sadly told us he did not have a dad. Ron immediately answered back, "Well, now you have a foster dad." "Forever?" Lamont pressed. "Yes, buddy, forever." To this day they still have a special relationship and share many interests through sports and hobbies. These times with Foster Dad are big bonding moments for both Ron and the children. Having a relationship with a positive male role model is one influence that will not fade as the years go by. Indeed, many children call Ron and me years later to ask for our advice or tell us of their successes.

Foster families can best fill a void in the life of a foster child if negative influences can be identified early before they have gotten a chance to get a hold of the children. Think about how many times we have all heard about unsupervised teens engaging in drug use or joining gangs as an attempt to fit in. Many do this because they are looking for friendship. Runaways can also fall victim to the dangerous world of trafficking while looking for acceptance and support. After all, the gang or pimp is a family of sorts, but certainly not a positive one. Therefore, we choose to be available to our foster children for emotional support even years down the line.

Though lifelong relationships are not a primary goal of foster caregiving, they frequently result from even a short time in foster care. We have had numerous young adults who were our foster children in the past contact us for moral support or advice years after leaving our home. Guidance given ranges from information on housing, finances, job hunting, and life counseling to finding a church to join and to offering support regarding marriages and a new generation of babies. The fierce bond of a permanent emotional connection is so special to be a part of because foster children, who come to us as strangers, nestle themselves into our hearts forever.

Relationships with the extended families of our foster children are another type of connection that can grow through foster care. Most family members sense being supported with their attempts to overcome their difficulties and be reunited with their children. In short, we sympathize with what the foster child and their family are going through and help them grow in strength and confidence in any way that is under our control. They usually appreciate the strong feelings of compassion and protection that the foster parents provide to their children. Good will and working toward a common goal of reunification help the two families form a truly unique bond.

When welcomed by the foster child's family, many biological parents choose to stay in touch with the foster family after reunification. This works out well because most foster families would never dream of abandoning the child after the placement ends. We have experienced Christmas cards, caroling parties, graduation celebrations, weddings, and christenings years after the official reunification day. Of course, every case is different, but having attachments with many of our foster children's families will allow the relationships to continue to flourish and are a hidden benefit to a life dedicated to others.

A young mom and dad whom we worked with years ago kindly still call from time to time to voluntarily check in and give us updates on their lives. While I cannot support all the aspects of their hectic life, I am cognizant in remembering that they are trying their best to care for their children within their means. When they call, it is a loud, energetic atmosphere heard through the phone, but the four children are always happy to chat (all at once), tell me about their school activities, and tattle on the other siblings.

One dear mother sends me the first-day-of-school pictures of her two children every year, even though I have not seen her girls in many years. She says every year on the first day of school the girls still like to reminisce about their foster family and the year they started school while at our home. Each September, school photos of numerous past foster children come through to my phone. It is such a blessing to be able to stay connected with our old "kiddos" and their families.

We have seen great friendships come from unconventional sources too. For example, we keep in contact with the grandmother of some of our most beloved children. Not only did she refer to me as "sister" the very first day we met, but she was always an advocate for me, her grandchildren, and the agency staff. This woman was a natural peacemaker. A nephew of hers did not approve of our family or the foster-care arrangement that the agency had decided upon, but as the matriarch of the family, she would not tolerate anything but respect among all the parties involved. I learned a great deal about confidence and leadership from her. This elder is still a positive role model and close friend of mine today.

We often find that the grandparents of our foster children become the ones who choose to keep in touch with us. We think this happens because of a sincere appreciation they have for our family and the interventions and safeguards we provided not only for their grandchildren but sometimes their children as well. They love their children and grandchildren both, but they are not blind to the struggles that are occurring. They thank us for taking their sons and daughters—the parents of our foster children—under our wing too. We have heard comments like, "We didn't know what to do with them when they were growing up." The care we provide for foster children is frequently helping more than one generation. Foster parents know that helping a needy child today may help prevent a broken adult tomorrow.

Great relationships also form when cultural differences are embraced amongst families. We have rarely witnessed anything but kindness behind a dozen different cultures. There are so many people who amplify differences, but we are here to tell you, as people who live it day to day, we do not often see it. We certainly do not see raising children from a culture different from our own as a roadblock. It is an opportunity for us all to share our unique perspectives. Of course, we have all had awkward experiences from those who make their nonverbal opinions known. However, we choose to not focus on these narrow-minded and unhealthy remarks. It is much easier to live life knowing all people are equally worth loving. God will sort out the rest later.

Recently, we did a ten-day respite for another foster family while they were out of town. Their six-month-old foster baby was a little hesitant around us because we were strangers to him. We usually have immediate connections to babies, but he seemed a little lost and sad. His foster family had darker skin tones than we do, but since he did not spend time looking in a mirror, we looked unfamiliar to him, even though we had the same complexion as he did. Since we keep many baby dolls with varying skin tones around the house, we had one that matched his foster family's complexion. It was so sweet when he saw the doll for the first time. He was immediately excited and happy, and he smiled, cooed, and flapped his arms in an attempt to reach out for her. Clearly the baby doll's skin tone was more familiar to him than ours and brought him comfort. Anytime he cried we snuggled with him and his baby doll, and each time we got that same darling, enthusiastic response. Talk about a great relationship!

Another day, I was in a hospital lobby with our six-month-old, handicapped foster child, Caleb. I was approached by a stranger who asked me if I was in favor of keeping handicapped children alive. What a shocking question! All lives are a gift from God. I wish that lady could have the opportunity to experience knowing handicapped children. They are extra joyful, resilient, and happy. They brightly radiate the image of God. Frankly, they may have more medical needs but they have far fewer behavioral issues. We feel that they are treasures to have placed in our home. In fact, when I was a young child, I remember asking my grandmother if she was sad that her son, my Uncle Tommy, had Down syndrome. In her sweet cheerful response, she said, "Oh no, Kathleen! He is my sunshine and never caused me a minute's trouble!" Then she winked at me and told me he was her favorite son. She had five sons . . . sorry, Dad.

Rock-solid relationships that form with fellow foster families are another highlight of fostering. Our emotional energy is sparked by working with people who see foster care in the same positive light we do and because we all understand the ups and downs of foster parenting. We have this unspoken code about keeping each other going. We build each other up when one is having a bad day, even if the bad day was only over spilled milk trickling down the floor vent. After all, this is real life, and little things do add up. We are all blessed to have been given this calling. Some days, we just have to remind each other.

One foster friendship comes to mind when I think about people who give us regular support. We had just had a new set of siblings placed with us. They were scared, nervous, and overwhelmed upon arrival to our house. Weeks passed in getting them settled in enough to catch a glimpse of their real personalities, but their level of need and energy remained as high as it was from the start. Patricia was having essentially the same situation at her house. We had two sets of foster siblings, and she had three sets! We often took turns babysitting to give the other a break. It took a great deal of veteran skill, energy, and ingenuity on both our parts to tackle all the issues both families were facing. Eventually, some of their nervous energy calmed. Patricia and I patted each other on the back that we survived that stressful year, and we reminisce about it often.

Friend relationships also quell loneliness, which is a legitimate complaint in the world of foster caregiving. People in vastly different roles within the foster-care world have shared feelings of loneliness, sometimes in a room full of people (or children). For example, families of foster children feel misunderstood, medical staffs are inundated with complaints, caseworkers have heavy caseloads, foster parents feel alone, police officers are made out to be the bad guys, and all levels of administrators are asked to do more with less. Foster care is often sad work, causing a large amount of turnover in both foster parents and agency personnel; quality friendships help battle the loneliness of the tough days.

Friends also help promote perseverance and optimism. You can either say, "I get to feed thirty-six meals today to the people I love" or "It's just another long day of cooking and cleaning." My friends and I actually do this, which makes me laugh out loud some days. Life is all about perspective, meaning some days require talking yourself into having a good day. We are reminded to be obsessively grateful for the opportunity to live our lives another day, keeping in mind that we have cared for foster children who cannot get out of bed unassisted, get dressed independently, or even eat by mouth.

Our peer foster-family friends are gifts from God. Their understanding hearts and enormous generosity are often what keep us going. Anything that seems impressive in this book is dull in comparison to the work of many of our fostering friends.

It would be impossible to mention every foster family we have come across in our years. Suffice it to say, their unselfish hearts and bright parenting ideas are an inspiration to our family.

Finally, countless relationships evolve with individuals outside the fostering circle. There are gracious people willing to bend over backward to help a foster family. There is our local pharmacist who answers endless questions, fields phone calls from the doctors' offices, and works magic with medical benefits. Our local community center staff accommodates the unique needs of our foster children regarding their programming activities. We have librarians who get to know our children's interests and help nourish their love of reading. Medical staff and counselors provide appointments and expertise for endless medical needs. Parishioners and neighbors cheerfully and sincerely welcome each child who comes through our home. Local dispatchers and police officers know of our home and mission. Dedicated teachers embrace the special circumstances of our foster children's lives every single day. Because of their helpful nature, these people make a significant impact on our fostering stamina.

The easiest way to grow as competent foster parents is to surround ourselves with people smarter and more experienced than we are. These invaluable relationships form a team that holds most of us to these tough service-oriented jobs day after day. They are our lifeline to keeping mentally healthy and emotionally strong so we can continue to be effective as we raise our foster children.

CHAPTER 8: SACRIFICES

The foster-care commitment centers around being ready for the job. The process to get a foster-care license is more than paperwork and a home study. Foster caregiving includes completely opening your heart and home to the vulnerabilities of the outside world. Foster parents endure profound sacrifices, but fostering is also the perfect opportunity to look outside ourselves and give back to others. Our family's motivational motto is "JOY," which stands for Jesus first, others second, yourself third.

Foster families weigh the benefits of providing a home for a needy child with the challenge of the daily pressures that it entails. We try our best to provide an excellent fostering experience for all the children who come through our home, but that does not mean every day is easy. One way of dealing with a seemingly unsolvable dilemma—possibly something we have not had previous experience with—is to ask another veteran foster parent for ideas. It is impossible to prepare ourselves for every situation because every child will bring new behaviors to the table. The differing behaviors create opportunities to brainstorm and learn from others. Jayne, being an experienced, ingenious, and creative foster mom, often comes up with a good consequence or a better safety measure if I am out of ideas. I help her with ideas too. This camaraderie helps ease the strain of the daily pressures and adds protection for not only the children, but for us as well.

We had a particularly challenging set of teens—Audrey, fifteen; Abigail, fourteen; and Adam, thirteen—who threw us a new curveball each day they were with us. Their response for any request was a long drawn out "ohhh" as if they had no idea what I was asking of them. Their ability to follow directions was nonexistent, which became very taxing when taking care of them over a long period of time. Our sanity was in jeopardy every day when we repeatedly had to ask the teens to complete simple tasks they should have known how to do. Daily, as we struggled to get them to leave the house for school on time, they would be on their school-issued laptops instead of brushing teeth, combing hair, and packing bags. They acted shocked that I asked them to do the same routine every day. I had had higher expectations for these teenagers to take initiative to get ready for school independently. At Jayne's suggestion, we altered the environment. To decrease our frustrations and promote their ability to prioritize tasks, we placed their computers in a locked chest each night to eliminate the distraction in the morning. The computers were placed in their backpacks just as they started out the door to walk to the bus stop. This adjustment got the attention of the teens and led to a better understanding of morning routines and expectations, mercifully resulting in less incredulous "ohhh" being heard.

One huge sacrifice of the foster-care world is a lack of privacy. There is scrutiny to be endured and real feelings of living in a glass house. People will criticize your individual parenting skills not realizing that the needs of foster children can be different from the needs of a normally developing child. There is uncertainty in how foster children will act in your home, what they will say, or how they will interpret your actions. Documentation efforts may or may not reflect what actually happened. The feelings of exposure and vulnerability are legitimate. Our handicapped foster son needed a full-time night nurse to monitor him because he stopped breathing so often. While this was a Godsend for his safety, it still felt like a lack of privacy having a nurse working in our home at night while we slept.

Other sacrifices of foster parenting include a lack of downtime. Foster care is a busy lifestyle, and new children can come in at any time. Regular family dynamics include all the usual routines; this is busy enough on its own. But life becomes increasingly involved, verging on overwhelming, when foster children are added. Personal leisure time is very limited. Busy does not necessarily mean bad, but the adjustment to a lack of downtime is often unexpected and takes getting used to.

Recently, three siblings—all of whom had different fathers—were placed with us. Over a one-month period we took in the three children, got them settled, clothed, taken to the doctor and registered for school and basketball. Then slowly, one by one, the children were granted placement with three different paternal relatives, and they all needed packed up again to be transferred out of our home. While it is good that the children are with family members, busy is still busy.

When we first became foster parents as a newly married couple, we found the lack of a steady schedule to be challenging. After accepting a foster child into our home, we were immediately thrown into this unfamiliar world of playdates, routine bedtimes, and having a need for approved babysitters. When the children went home, we were back to being a childless couple that was invited out to evening events again. The situation was odd and felt like we were living in two different worlds.

Foster families who take in a long-term foster child from the start may not notice the ups and downs of this busy revolving door as much as those who have several short-term placements in a row. Short-term foster placements will have days centered around constant intake appointments aimed at stabilizing the child. Just as one set of children gets their intake medical, dental, and vision appointments completed, they move on to an acceptable kinship placement or sometimes even go home. Another set of children may come in, sometimes on the same day!

One day, I took a set of my most cherished foster children— Dante, Aisha, Clyde, and Marie—to be reunified with their biological family. Through many tears, I managed to hand them off to the agency staff and walk sadly back to my car. As I was getting ready to put my car in reverse, my phone rang with a new set of little ones, Tre and Gabby, who would also become two of my most memorable foster children. I barely had a minute to catch my breath before I was saying yes to this new set of children. Normally I would not accept children back-to-back like this, but maybe God knew I needed this blessing to ease my broken heart.

Foster families make the sacrifice of accepting that their schedules cannot be set in stone. Calls to consider the placement of foster children come at the most unusual times and never when you are sitting on the couch relaxed and ready with all your work done. One call we received was on the evening of the best NBA championship ever—the Cleveland Cavaliers winning in 2016! Practically everyone in Northeast Ohio was headed to celebration parties. The placement worker on the other end of the phone pleaded for us to consider two children, Lyndsey and Jacob, who were sitting in the agency lobby waiting for a foster home to be found. She was having problems getting other potential foster families to answer their cell phones that night. Our NBA party would have to wait so the tired little sister and brother could finally leave the agency after a long day and go home with us.

Altering our schedule at the last minute happens frequently. We have learned to be mindful of asking a new foster child to sit still for an important event, such as an awards banquet or music performance. We found this out the hard way many years ago at our teens' Christmas concert, which was also the day Chris arrived. He decided he was going to have a long, loud, disruptive temper tantrum in the middle of the school auditorium. There was no comforting him. Our only option was to sacrifice our leisure time and cut the evening short. A better approach would have been to call on a foster parent peer or alternative caregiver to watch our new, spirited child that night. Unfortunately, it all happened so fast it left little time for preparation.

Since then, we have learned to not take a new child to any formal event on their first few evenings in care. I have learned to schedule what I call "ghost babysitters." I ask my alternative caregivers to keep a certain important date open just in case I would have a foster child that day. One weekend, we had two events planned: an academic ceremony on Friday and a charity event on Saturday. While we had no foster children at that time, we planned ahead in case we did get a fostering call. We had two different ghost babysitters set up for that weekend, one on each night, as a precaution. These people are always so dear to understand our unusual circumstances and cheerfully pencil us onto their calendar in case we have a last-minute need.

Lack of sound sleep is also a major sacrifice—and for several reasons. First, foster parents almost have to learn to sleep with their eyes open in anticipation of possible mischievous behavior. Years ago, we had a foster child whom we developed safety concerns about regarding our newborn baby. One evening, through the baby monitor, we heard a rustling of items in our baby's crib and heard our eight-year-old foster child, Maya—whom we discovered (after she was already placed in our home) had a history of being severely sexually abused—sneaking around our child's bedroom. The noise was occurring long after we had checked that Maya was asleep. We were told we could not put a baby monitor in Maya's bedroom because of privacy issues for her. So instead, we put one next to our child's crib and hid another one out of sight on the floor under the crib. We are not sure what Maya's intention was, but after that incident we moved the baby into our room for the six-month duration Maya stayed with us.

The second reason lack of sleep is such a major sacrifice for foster parents is because the "sleeping-through-the-night job" is never done. Once Ron and I got our one-, two-, and three-year-old foster children to consistently sleep through the night, they went home. That is great for their family, but to us that meant new children to train to sleep through the night. After those three children left, we took in a handicapped baby who needed tube feeds every three hours around the clock. When he left, twin one-year-olds arrived. While we are truly blessed with all these children, the sleep sacrifices are grueling.

Sleep sacrifices affect the other members of the house too. Good communication about children coming in and out of the home is needed to keep everyone informed about foster children arriving, even if it occurs in the middle of the night. We would often go into our own children's bedrooms late at night to let them know new children had arrived in the house. By keeping our family notified, we ensured that no one was caught off guard or frightened seeing someone unexpected in the house at night. One night many years ago, Matthew tripped over a cot in his room on his way to the bathroom. He had not remembered me waking him earlier and telling him there was a boy in his room until we could get another twin bed out of storage the next day.

When Matthew was away at college, he was caught off guard late one night as he watched an unknown, husky male stumbling around our front door at 1am. Matthew had received a notification from our smart doorbell and didn't realize the man who was slipping on the icy surface of the porch was a social worker dropping off a new set of foster children. He had missed the video footage of the carload of children being delivered to the house a few minutes prior. Once I finally picked up my phone, he told me he was about to call the police thinking this unfamiliar man was an intruder. We now remember to call or text our adult children if new foster children are coming into care late at night. Foster caregiving still requires constant adjustments for all our family members.

Other privacy limitations that foster families encounter are having staff members from various agencies visiting throughout the month. People will know your daily household business, and they will also repeatedly inspect every room in your home. There are visits from the foster child's caseworker as well as a different caseworker who oversees the foster home itself (sometimes called the foster-care coordinator). There may be therapists, teachers, and attorneys who might visit several times a month. We also disclose the time frames that we are out of town, so the agency nighttime placement staff knows when we are unavailable to take in emergency placements. These are all part of the lack of privacy that foster parents endure.

Revealing private family finances is an unconventional part of the foster-parent sacrifice. The rationale given by the agency for this practice is to determine that the foster family has sufficient funds to support their family without adding in the foster-care reimbursement stipend. The agency provides stipend reimbursement checks to subsidize the increased expenses incurred while foster children are in the home, but reimbursement checks are not considered sufficient funds to solely raise the child, even for a short time. Foster parents are volunteers, and reimbursements are not salary. Some amount of personal money is going to be used to support foster children, so being financially prepared is necessary.

Probably the feelings of isolation and violation of privacy are most vivid when an allegation occurs. An allegation is a complaint or grievance not yet proven to be true. If you are in the business long enough, allegation investigations are likely to be a part of your foster home's history. This is a sacrifice that is both nerve-racking and scary. One seven-year-old girl, whose foster mother turned the little girl's chin toward her when she spoke, immediately said, "You're choking me!" Her older brother sitting next to her instantly said to his sister, "No, she didn't." The foster mom quickly suspected that this child would bring the incident up to her counselor or caseworker in the coming weeks. The foster mom documented and notified the agency about the "choking" comment immediately. Shortly after the communication with the agency, the child mentioned the incident to a counselor, and the anticipated allegation process began. The foster mom knew what she did was not rough and was intended to teach the child the important skill of eye contact. This allegation investigation was then opened and closed quickly and found to be unsubstantiated (not true). However, even a small incident like this will initiate weeks of investigation, stress, and silence on the part of the agency staff while they collect and assess the facts. This foster mom stated that, though the investigation was readily dropped, the process greatly upset her and seemed like an insult to her parenting skills.

Another allegation incident happened when a foster mother was using the bathroom. During this time, an older foster child who was at her home on respite hit a younger foster child already placed with her. The next day the younger foster child developed a bruise. When asked, both the older and younger foster children gave the same explanation as to what happened, but the foster home was still found guilty of neglect. Explaining the neglect charge to the foster mom, the placing agency said it had wanted the older child to be completely separated from the other children when she was not in immediate eyesight. The foster mother had not been made aware of this expected level of care when she took the child in on respite. Sadly, this veteran family elected to end their twenty-year foster-care career on this negative note after a long and trying allegation process.

These grossly public moments shake the resolve of foster families. Negative events like these are reasons why some foster parents quit. The sacrifice is just too great. The painful reality is that any child can say anything about you and your home on any given day. Children will sometimes process what happened differently from what the adults meant or may make claims in a purposeful effort to get removed from the home. There are also times when children are coached by members of their own family to retaliate against the foster parents. Keeping the happenings in the home as transparent as possible, openly sharing any questionable incidents immediately up the chain of command, and maintaining meticulous documentation are the best safeguard defenses.

There are many other hidden sacrifices, such as the time given up with your own biological children, friends, and aging parents. If I cannot find an alternative caregiver for my newly placed foster child on the night of my biological child's birthday dinner out at a restaurant, I will have to miss the event and stay home so as not to put the foster child in an overwhelming situation or to detract from my bio child's evening. I rarely schedule lunches with friends because the likelihood of me canceling the engagement is high. I struggle to come to terms with the time missed with my aging parents. On the other hand, I have wonderful memories of my late mother feeding so many foster babies through the years, with the sweetest loving smile on her face, and I absolutely remember to treasure every second I get to spend with my dad. Foster parents selflessly donate these precious years of their lives to serve others.

Fostering brings many sacrifices because it is a 24/7/365 job. Adjusting to the privacy issues, the lack of downtime, our constantly changing schedule, and the risk of allegations are some of the sacrifices all foster parents make. I have heard social workers, police officers, nurses, doctors, and teachers say they could not be a foster parent. Though I believe this comment is meant as a compliment, it does not alleviate the fact that many more quality foster homes are needed to service the nearly half-million children in our country living in "out-of-home placements." Even though the sacrifices are great, most of us still would not trade this experience for the world.

CHAPTER 9: MENTAL PREPAREDNESS

The key to successful foster parenting is having foster parents who are realistically prepared for the journey. While no one has a perfect home, and no one needs to be a perfect parent, individuals interested in foster care should be in good shape emotionally and mentally. Foster parents hear about but do not fully process the level of inner strength needed for long-term success in foster caregiving. This idealism is a reason some foster parents fail. Other types of volunteer work require a few hours a day or a few days a week, whereas the constant service of foster caregiving rarely stops.

Ron and I consider being a rock-solid support person to each other serious business. We must be on the same page about taking in foster children because mental stresses are too draining if mutual support for each other is not in place. We both have our gifts, and while we can adequately handle each other's chores and responsibilities, it is not always pretty. We choose to divide up household duties. I typically take care of foster-care paperwork, appointments, schooling, daycare, and medicines. Ron handles financials, insurance, donations, and vacations. We share childcare, religious, and extracurricular activity commitments.

As stated, fellow foster-parent support is the strongest factor in promoting mental preparedness. We completely understand each other's needs and stresses and will move heaven and earth to help one another. One day, a fellow foster mom called me and stated she needed a place for her five kiddos to go that entire day, just because she was feeling so overwhelmed. That statement is enough of an explanation for any foster mom to agree to immediately help because we have all experienced those difficult days ourselves. Within an hour, her five children had arrived, our schedules were dropped, and one small act of kindness commenced. Society would like to have every foster-care arrangement be always wonderfully happy, but the truth is we all have meltdowns - foster children and foster parents alike.

Another time, a foster mom called to say that she had just been notified that an infant sibling to her current foster toddler had been born two days prior. The baby was coming into foster care from the hospital that very day. She had not even known that the mom of her toddler had been expecting, as the woman was incarcerated. Still, the foster mom and her family decided to take the newborn in without any previous preparation. She explained that she needed to go to the hospital right away for the newborn's discharge instructions. The toddler immediately arrived to spend the day with us, and by the end of the evening the infant had joined their family. Foster parents' superpower is to be completely flexible and supportive, even with little notice.

Family support is critically important to staying strong mentally in the foster-care journey. I cannot imagine getting through the day-to-day stresses of being a foster parent without the unwavering support of family and friends. We have received support in the form of meals, donations, and mother's helper support hours when a new baby arrives. We have family members who make all the difference in whittling down our chore and maintenance lists with their time and talents. We have had lovely gifts provided for the foster children for birthday and holiday occasions. The amount of supportive phone calls, texts, and good deeds our extended family gives is priceless and helps keep up our mental strength.

Being organized is crucial to mental preparedness. Staying on top of our own family's needs and appointments keeps our stress under control. Since there is rarely prior knowledge of a child coming into foster care, foster parents must be mentally prepared and ready all the time. When a new child does arrive, there will be a lot of running around and important appointments to tend to, and personal needs will be secondary, at least for a while. When I was actively working in the hospital at night as an RN, Ron would relay placement calls to me as I was tending to a full team of patients. After ten years on the night shift, I had to stop working those hours because I was unable to get the proper rest needed to mentally care for both foster children (who came at the drop of a hat) and hospital patients.

Our medically fragile foster son Caleb had 100 appointments in the first thirty-three days with us because he was so very sick. The hectic schedule of constant appointments takes an extra dose of stamina and commitment to get through. This high-stress time took a solid team effort on the part of Ron and me to keep our own household running. On days like these, we reminded each other that the hard work of foster caregiving does not happen on a specific timetable, and we need strong determination to weather the especially high-need times together.

Believe it or not, part of being mentally prepared also means being prepared for increased paperwork. Repeatedly completing the required documentation forms for foster children can seem overwhelming and taxing. Most folks contemplating the foster-care world do not think much about the added paperwork commitment. I find that scheduling routine time every day to work on documentation helps keep the time demands under control. In my experience, I have found that if my personal life is in good order before foster children are brought into the mix, I can stay on top of their multiplying needs and still keep my home running efficiently too.

Good health habits are also part of our routine to keep us strong for the mental rigors of the fostering job. This includes eating well, exercising, and acknowledging the importance of taking care of our own medical needs. Parents often fail in this area because they are busy taking care of others' needs. Making it a priority to take good care of ourselves helps Ron and me take better care of others. To that end, Ron and I go for a daily walk to care for both our physical and mental health. Sometimes just the two of us take our highly energetic dog, Jack. Other times we have children along. We use these walks to mentally decompress, catch up on the day's events, and tackle our 10,000 steps together.

Sergeant—a preteen respite placement—had been living in a world of chaos. He seemed to only know how to live his days attracting attention with his endless negative behaviors. He lacked direction and focus and did not get along with his peers. While in our home, he picked fights and caused damage to toys, walls, and just about everything in between. His antics were draining. He frequently commented on how our family walks relaxed him, even though from our point of view his energy level never slowed a bit. He could run up and down the street three times and climb four trees before we got within ear shot of him! He would examine every leaf, rock, and stick and still have time for great conversations with us in between. These were the best moments with this fella because we saw his curious nature and his intense interest in the world around him. We took this time to refill our emotional cup in the evenings, which gave us the strength to parent him during the days.

I know a string of foster moms with health concerns of their own who put off treatment because being a foster parent is so time-consuming. They put their needs last and delayed their medical attention until they were in between placements. Likewise, many aging foster parents want to retire but feel that they cannot because of the lack of adequate numbers of foster homes. We have to not only take good care of the foster homes we have but also encourage new families to be disciplined regarding the importance of their own health needs before they start this mission.

Part of mental readiness regarding fostering is having a cooperative and positive attitude. An upbeat disposition helps the children feel more at ease, helps the caseworkers have a more enjoyable job, and makes everyone more pleasant to be around. Obviously, we have our share of very difficult days in foster care. For instance, we got a call one day that our five foster children were leaving, court ordered, in an hour. This call came out of the blue with no time to prepare the children and no time to say goodbye. We were all stunned, but digging deep emotionally, we smiled and were upbeat and spent our last few minutes telling them how proud we were of their efforts in foster care, how we wanted them to remember the life skills and safety measures they had learned, and that we would always remember them and pray for their family daily. We know that leaving the children with our portrayed positivity and best wishes was what they needed on that terrible day.

As expected, foster children will tell their parents about life in foster care. No matter their age, all foster children easily catch on to the prevailing attitude of the foster home, whether it is generally negative or positive in nature. We want children to grow up in a happy environment. While information about the parents and the details of the cases are often difficult, we make our best effort to remain positive. Each foster child's family is unique, and while I do not excuse the poor circumstances that brought the children into foster care, I know many of these problems result from difficult circumstances, including poor upbringings of the family members themselves. We try to always speak kindly and with respect when referring to the foster children's families because it is very important for the children to hear this and will go a long way in developing a relationship with the child's family.

Mental strength means being able to compartmentalize the details of the abuse and neglect so the needs of the child, not the wrongs of the child's family, can be the focus. We try not to worry about the parts of the child's case that are out of our control. It is severely troubling to process the rape of a baby, to know that a child was forced to actively participate in pornography or prostitution, or to see an infant screaming inconsolably from the effects of drug exposure during pregnancy. The best way to deal with the difficult stresses is to try to have a forgiving heart because, frankly, it is not about us. God takes care of the judgment stuff. We channel our energy instead on taking excellent care of the children and providing love and compassion. We also fervently pray for good decision-making skills for the agency staff and court officials who will be making the rulings in the child's case.

One particularly troubling case involved monumental neglect. Four-year-old Destin was skin and bones when he arrived. His malnutrition was profound. He could not eat without vomiting because he was used to having a nearly empty stomach. His eyes were dull, vision nearly blind, and teeth full of holes. He was minimally verbal, had slow thought processes, big anger management problems, and was scared of his own shadow. His attorney was more concerned about his notorious winning record for parents than understanding the profound needs of the child. In the end, we were speechless and dumbfounded as Destin returned home. Obviously, we pray constantly for this boy while we work on resolving our feelings of anger, sadness, helplessness, and disappointment in this case. (We did hear sometime later that he went back into foster care and was placed in an adoptive home with a mother who was a schoolteacher for developmentally delayed children. Blessed prayers answered!)

In this line of work, we believe that we must forgive the wrongs the children have previously experienced. We have trained ourselves to step back from the raw emotions of the child's case and focus instead on being a tenacious advocate for the child by taking excellent care of them every day they are in our care. Foster parents do not make decisions about the case plan, but we have to find a way to live with the plan. Foster parents may be given a chance to speak in court, but in my experience, that is simply a formality. If we do not forgive, our emotional strength is quickly drained, and we would not want to be foster parents any longer. Fostering is not for the faint of heart; it takes courage and tenacity to stay.

We have also come to realize that a huge aspect of mental readiness is having faith. Faith gives us strength for our convictions. The closer we live to God the easier it is to see the needs of others, and the further we live from God the harder it is to want to do for others because we are too busy doing for ourselves. This is a great lesson to remember.

Many children have an interest in faith, but most have not been encouraged to pursue the journey. When we take foster children to church, some make comments such as, "I remember my grandma taking me to church like this when I was little" or "I know that prayer." The ones who already know about God usually embrace going back to church because they remember attending as part of their history. We teach our children that Jesus is their guide and will be their forever friend. We constantly emphasize that the joy they feel when making a good decision is Jesus inspiring them. We can only imagine what a comfort it is to a (frequently lonely) child to know they have a constant companion who is always with them.

Those children who have never been exposed to God are intrigued by the idea. Explaining God and the concept of going to church in a way children can understand can be challenging. We keep our explanations simple and explain that God is love. Anything good, happy, or joyful in the world comes from God. From there, their faith builds naturally. Our intent is not to convert them but to always help children feel loved, supported, and comforted.

Jamal came from an exceptionally abusive and neglectful environment. He witnessed frequent domestic violence incidents and endured daily beatings. We talked with him about Jesus and taught him how God guides us if we listen to our conscience. This fella had never heard of Jesus before coming to our home, but eventually he started to say bedtime prayers on his own. He even became more aware of the good and bad choices he was making and would comment that "Jesus helped me decide what to do." When he left to go to an adoptive home, he asked me where he could get a prayer card of Jesus like the one in his room. He gave me a big hug when I gave him that prayer card to take along with him. I told him that Jesus was with him wherever he went, whether he had a prayer card or not. There is not a day that goes by that I do not think of this beloved child and his special prayer card.

Mental toughness is the basis to being a solid foster parent. Paying attention to our own needs will keep us strong, which allows our attention to shift to little ones with big needs. We encourage ourselves and others to not compare one person's life to another because we have no idea what their journey was all about. So, we do our job keeping the goal of healing and strengthening children in the forefront of our minds. This includes being proactive in keeping ourselves physically, mentally, and spiritually healthy and always taking our daily walk.

CHAPTER 10: PHYSICAL READINESS

Preparing a foster home takes thought, time, and money. Foster children have many conflicting feelings running through their minds when they come into foster care. In turn, we strive to have a calm and comfortable home ready to receive them. Their intake day (the day they come into the custody of the state) has likely been filled with stress, sadness, and frightening changes. By having our house physically ready ahead of time, we will have additional time to deal with those worries and concerns that first day.

When initially preparing our home for foster children, we kept in mind our ideal foster-child placement, but we knew the reality was that we were likely to be asked to take other ages of children too. There are families that love to care for newborns (one peer just took in her 75th!) and others that will consider every age but an infant. Babies under eight weeks of age cannot go to daycare, and all children under the age of twenty-four months must sleep in a crib of their own. We asked ourselves if we were willing to buy two cribs to accommodate siblings who were ten and twenty months old (yes) or three cribs to accommodate triplets (no). Each of these scenarios takes thought when deciding how to set up a foster-care space.

One day, a call was going around for triplet newborns. Many of us in the foster-care community declined the request, as we did not have the space and beds to accommodate three cribs. I eventually heard that an Amish family had three cribs available and was able to accept those newborns into their home. What a blessing for those tiny siblings to be able to stay in foster care together.

Keeping siblings together absolutely takes a great deal of commitment from the placement staff at the agency and the foster family alike, but the importance of keeping related children together cannot be overemphasized. Since only a brother, sister, or close cousin can truly understand the experiences of their life, the related children staying together in the same foster home can help each adjust to the experience. Typically, if they can be placed in foster care together, they suffer fewer disrupted placements, fewer behavioral problems, and do not have the added stress of feeling the need to search for siblings later. Statistically, two-thirds to three-fourths of foster children have a sibling in foster care also.[7]

We once took in a baby, Jessa, from the hospital. The darling baby was addicted to drugs because her mother used heroin, fentanyl, and other substances while pregnant with her. Jessa suffered months and months of difficult withdrawal symptoms.

Later, as she was transitioning into an adoptive home, a previously unknown brother, Eddie, was found in the basement of a drug home in a nearby county. Once Eddie was taken into foster care in that neighboring county, per protocol, the officials from both counties conferred and eventually got the two siblings adopted together in the same home. The adoptive parents were not originally looking to adopt two children but changed their plan to happily accept the sibling too. Many foster and adoptive parents alter their original plans and bed space to support the very important sibling bond.

Next with our preparedness plan is considering how to make our home safe. As professional parents, our obligation is to ensure as safe an environment as possible. As careful as we are with our own children, there is additional weight that comes from parenting a child who is not our own. All children deserve to have a foster home that is in good repair, clean, and safe. Our foster-care state licensure requires this of course, but more importantly, we want to take excellent care of these children who have already endured so much hardship in their young lives.

Books and other types of media almost always portray foster homes as old and rundown with unpleasant foster parents and little food or toys. There are slimy rodents and filthy yards with dilapidated buildings. I have been to many foster homes and have never witnessed a space like this. I sincerely hope that foster care has evolved enough over time to debunk these narratives. Keeping the foster home in a state of good repair is the goal of most foster parents.

To ensure that our home is as safe as possible, I ask our town's fire marshal to come to our house every few years, even though this is not required, for an informal walk-through. He points out potential trouble spots I may miss or discloses a rule that may have changed. One such comment he made recently was the need for the electrical panel door on the fuse box to be always firmly latched to prevent an electrical charge from jumping from the box to a nearby carpet or couch and possibly starting a fire. We are thankful he pointed out this potential hazard. Who knew? Just when you think every plug in your house has a childproof cover, a new electrical socket grows out of the wall during the inspection.

We look at all areas of our home with a child's eye. We try to identify safety concerns from their point of view and curiosity level. We secure large pieces of furniture to walls to prevent an active child from pulling it onto themselves, and we ensure that electrical cords, chemicals, and cleaning supplies are out of reach and in a locked cabinet. Knives and scissors will need to be secured for some foster children, and a locked medication area will be needed for all. Any firearm must be unloaded, locked, and inaccessible to the children. Our license requires that, on each floor of the home, we have both fire and carbon monoxide detectors, which must be checked at least twice a year by agency staff to make sure they are updated and working. Fire escape routes and tornado evacuation meeting areas also have to be pictorially posted on each floor.

We once had a set of five teen siblings that warranted us needing to use a footlocker with a padlock each night to lock in our knives, scissors, medicines, laptops, wallets, and purses because of their after-hours mischievousness. This was our earnest attempt to keep them safe. In reality though, there are all sorts of items in a home that could be used with malintent if wanted. In addition to the footlocker, we worked diligently on constant communication and helping them see themselves as worthwhile individuals. We emphasized looking toward a world after foster care where they would be searching for jobs and employment. We worked to improve their decision-making skills and explained that choices they made today would have a big effect on what happened in their lives in the future. We promoted hope for a better future by encouraging them to make peace with their past so it would not spoil their present or future. Having hopes and dreams are better safeguards than a hundred locks.

Since nighttime can be filled with concerns and worries for foster parents, we secure valuables and set up baby gates, monitors, and magnetic chimes on doors and windows as needed so we can hear if a little one (or a big one) gets out of bed for midnight roaming. These tools will aid in a better night's sleep for all members of the foster home. Withstanding the rigors of the foster-care world depends on your ability to creatively help these children, all while not putting your own safety and health at risk. Part of this means modifying day-to-day routines to keep the foster children and the other household members safe, while also finding a way to get a decent night's rest.

Three little boys—Joe (six), Billy (four), and Nelson (three)—came into our care one evening. After they were settled into bed, Nelson climbed over the gate separating the boys' room from the nearby staircase. We found him downstairs by the front door trying to open the lock. He stated he was going home. We were worried he would try again and might succeed at getting out if we went to sleep. We ended up stacking a second gate on top of the first for added safety those first few nights. We knew that he could easily push the gates out into the hall, but the crash would at least be noisy enough to wake us. We thought we were being creative, but instead he said he liked the gates because they made him feel safe. He went right to sleep and did not try to leave again. Within a week, he was settled into a bedtime routine, and we took the gates down.

Teen Kaye was untrustworthy regarding limits set on our personal possessions. She chose to sneak around at night and get into items she had been told were off limits. We finally put a magnetic chiming doorbell on the outside of her bedroom door. If needed, she could go to the bathroom, but the chime did sound alerting us she was up. We checked that she went back to bed in a reasonable amount of time and reset the alarm. In just one night, this solved the problem of her nighttime rummaging because she was embarrassed that the other children in the house knew she was out of bed. Eventually we built enough trust in her that we could leave the chime deactivated. The idea is to stop the unwanted behavior by working smarter not harder.

Another part of physical readiness is to build up a supply inventory. For years, we have run an informal consignment shop out of our basement. We keep various totes filled with quality clothes that we have found through store clearances, garage sales, and hand-me-down donations from friends.

Numerous foster families share their clothes with each other by dividing up donations they receive. We have totes with all sizes of shoes, socks, boots, hats, and gloves for the children to use. We also keep a variety of pacifiers, baby bottles, and formulas that are rotated to keep fresh. A supply of pillows, linens, blankets, and assorted-sized coats are a must.

Elizabeth and I frequently work to inventory and store the items so they are ready at a moment's notice. We stock bikes, toys, and the occasionally coveted electronic device. The never-ending hunt for a bargain is a necessity to keep the hidden financial demands under control. Foster parents are thrilled to find a nice bike at a garage sale because we want to send a bike, helmet, and a nice supply of toys with the children when they go back to their family. The hunt to repeatedly replace unexpired baby equipment, toys, games, and quality shoes and clothing is constant depending on the age of the child leaving, as well as the next one coming into our care.

In a coincidental turn of events, one day Ron brought home a large linen donation from a coworker consisting of many pillows, blankets, and sheets. Initially I thought that I did not need all the items donated, but that very night a call came in with a request to place six children. Talk about divine intervention! The children were nervous and scared when they arrived, and having fresh linens, plush pillows, and cute stuffed animals on each bed helped them feel a little more comfortable. Children will remember the first few hours at your home when they were in their most vulnerable state.

Clothing vouchers provided by the placing agency are typically brought with the child at the time of placement. These funds will be used to purchase clothes, shoes, and coats for the children to use during their time in foster care and beyond. Our stock of donations helps fill in the gaps that the clothing vouchers do not cover. At present, the vouchers are a one-time payment that ranges from $200-$250, depending on the age of the child and the season of the year. Most agencies work the rest of the ongoing clothing allowance into the daily reimbursement stipend. Anyone who shops for clothes knows coats, boots, underpants, and a couple of outfits quickly take up the full amount of the clothing voucher and will not cover all the items children need as they grow and mature while in foster care.

Some foster parents state that the reimbursement covers the daily amount of increased food, laundry soap, electric bills, etc.; however, having the child truly live at your home as a full-fledged family member costs more. Even if you reconcile yourself to the fact that you are providing care at a volunteer's rate, you still must factor in the expenses of birthday parties, pool passes, eating out after Sunday church, and many other miscellaneous expenses. Most foster parents try hard to treat their foster children as they do their own and want to provide these fun childhood extras.

One night, I had just sat down on my bed to turn on the 11pm news when my phone rang. I recognized the number as the nighttime placement worker's cell. I remember picking up the phone and joking with her saying, "Mary, how did you know that I just sat down and put my feet up?" She half chuckled and half apologized and then went on to explain that two children were found in a car not far from our home. The mother had been revived from a drug overdose by the police. She wanted to know if there was any way we could take in these two children, whom they knew almost nothing about. Simultaneously, I heard a car door slam shut outside my bedroom window. I looked out, and there was the worker and children in the driveway! She said that she knew I would say yes, so they were already on their way—well yes, apparently so! The baby was wearing nothing but a dirty diaper, and a paramedic had thrown a small medical blanket over her. Her eighteen-month-old sister was only wearing a soiled pajama shirt and a diaper. Talk about a last-minute need for a supply of pacifiers, pajamas, and formula!

Since we often foster sibling groups, we keep several sizes of beds on hand to accommodate babies to teenagers. We have stationary-sided cribs, as drop-side crib rails are no longer considered safe or allowed by our license for children under two. Extra beds are needed because we never know when a child in our preferred age range will come with other siblings we want to keep together. We also stock a line of car seats in our garage that we check frequently to ensure they have not expired. Car seats expire because plastic on the car seats can be weakened by repeated temperature changes or simply over time. If the car seat is ever in a car accident, it is immediately thrown away as an added precaution. This goes for bike helmets too.

Foster homes need a variety of toys to entertain a variety of personalities and ages. Children's enjoyment comes from being kept busy by working toys that are appropriate for their age and development. We also like to have many gross motor toys to keep children's bodies and minds occupied. We steer away from the never-ending video game trap, though the children do play with them at controlled times. We prefer interactive and outdoor play, such as splash pools, sprinklers, sled riding, or time on the swing set. Social workers tell stories of the foster children's original homes where there are only broken toys lying around. We like to organize toys with small parts in gallon-sized bags so they are always intact and clean, with all parts in good-working order. Children find this to be a real treat.

One set of three sisters—Caroline, Lucy, and Vivi—were mesmerized with our toy room. They were thrilled with the variety of toys. Developmentally they were very different. Vivi was a two-year-old who acted like an average two-year-old. Lucy was a five-year-old who was the mature parentified child. Caroline was thirteen years old and had significant developmental delays; therefore, she needed toddler-level activities that fit her mature teenage size. Caroline liked the swings and play mats, Lucy was engrossed with the kitchen set and ironing board, and Vivi toddled around on the scooters. They each found something that was just right for their interest, size, and development. At the end of the two-week respite, they said they did not want to leave. Lucy reluctantly put all the pieces of each toy carefully back together in the assigned bags and told me, "Foster Mom, you have very nice toys." It still makes me chuckle as I remember how serious her mature comment sounded.

To accommodate young sibling groups, we stock duplicates of our most used pieces of baby equipment. We have had many sets of siblings that are ten to twelve months apart or twins who used two cribs, two highchairs, and two swings. Unbelievably, one family we were called about had three sets of twins—ages four, two, and newborn! There are many multiples in foster care, so we use all our supplies time and time again.

Being physically prepared to take in foster children long term means I am cognizant of the wear and tear on our home, which can be disheartening at times. I prepare for the fact that almost every area of our house will take a daily beating. The ripped books, smashed toys, broken video games, and items stolen throughout the years are too numerous to count. My general rule when buying carpeting, draperies, or furniture is to search for materials that "wear like burlap." The couch will get thrown up on, spilled on, and wet through, so I try buying leather, which is durable and washes well. I decorate with valances, as curtains will surely be used as a tissue for little noses and will be repeatedly pulled down.

One foster child, Danielle, picked an area of wallpaper off the wall in the kitchen while I had gone to the basement to check on another child. In just a few minutes, she quickly pulled many small and long strips of wallpaper off and shredded them into tiny pieces ensuring no possibility of repair. Since we had no replacement paper, the wall stood bare for years. Tre and Gabby stuffed toys under the sump pump lid while playing in the basement. This caused a $3,000 repair for the burning up of two commercial-grade motors. After this, we immediately added a permanent wall to keep the children away from the area.

Over the years, we have learned to buy and keep equipment when we see it, then rotate the items in and out of storage to fit our current children's needs. This approach keeps excessive clutter in our house to a minimum. Foster parents have told many stories of cleaning frenzies before caseworkers come to visit! One fond memory of some old friends makes me laugh. The foster mom was quickly tidying up the kitchen before a short-notice visit from her foster child's caseworker. Hastily, she gathered a bunch of dirty dishes and toys and put them into the microwave. During the visit the caseworker asked if she could help get the baby's bottle ready. The foster mom's initial reaction was "sure," but then she immediately remembered what she had done. It was too late! The microwave had already been opened and the mess revealed.

As time passes, we all get more comfortable with having foster children in and out of our homes. There will be little time, if any, to run to the store, buy a crib, and get it set up before a child comes through the door. We plan ahead as much as possible to get the children comfortably welcomed and settled into a well-prepared foster home. A new normal starts to evolve over time, and the everyday status of our home balances.

CHAPTER 11: THE DAY YOU'VE BEEN WAITING FOR

There is quite a significant period of time that passes from the moment a family commits to starting their foster caregiving dream to the day when their first foster child is standing in their kitchen. By this point, new foster parents have been anticipating this call so long that they can let the feelings in their heart rather than the knowledge in their head influence their decision to take a child in. I want to explain why the first call to take a foster child placement is extremely important for the child, the foster family, and the community as well.

Foster parents are frequently caught off guard when being contacted with a placement call for a foster child. Rarely is a preplanned time set for the removal of the children from their homes, and more often, calls come in with an immediate request for placement within an hour or two. When the call comes in, we are thoughtful with our decision and remain

113

mindful of the type of child we planned for. We do not allow ourselves to be guilted into a foster-child placement that has not been adequately contemplated or that we have major reservations about. Further, we encourage new families to consider waiting a year or two before venturing away from their initial predetermined age comfort zone. Over time, as a strong knowledge develops regarding this special type of parenting, foster families are more likely to succeed in caring for a wider age range of children. The placement call with the decision that follows has a trickle-down effect on a wide demographic.

Every placement call for a child signals us to pause, listen attentively to the information, ask good questions, and give serious thought to the consequences of the answer given. Whether a foster child seems like a good fit or not, we ask to take a few minutes to think about the call before giving a well-thought-out answer. Many times, the most hesitant acceptances can also end up being the most rewarding placements. Understand that if the answer is no, the guilty feelings will set in. All foster parents feel it, both new and veteran. If the answer is yes, cold feet may set in, but this feeling will eventually pass. Remember, the decision made will affect the neighborhood, the school system, and the community you live in. Therefore, the initial decision is crucial.

No one wants to say no to a placement, but it is better for children to be placed correctly the first time around rather than having to move later because of the inability of the foster home to meet their specific needs. The push to place children is fueled by the desire to find a home to accept them as quickly as possible. To preserve their stability and bonding, we want to avoid having to move children unnecessarily. Getting the placement match right initially means less chance of disruptions, for the children and the foster home, and saves the county money and man hours in the end.

We also keep in mind that anything can happen between the time the placement phone call comes in and the time the child arrives. From our experience, we have learned that, until the whites of the child's eyes are seen here in our home, we do not count on the child definitely coming. Foster-care placements fall through all the time, and oftentimes you will not even be notified. There is a traumatic situation happening at the child's home, the agency, the courthouse, or the police station, so it is a rare occasion when great communication among all parties happens. For a couple of years, I kept stats as to the calls we received for the placement of children and how many actually came to our home. Twenty-five to thirty-seven percent was the range of times the children we said yes to never ended up coming. So, until they arrive, we keep our feelings in check.

All those years ago, after we found out our foster-parent license was approved, we sat waiting for several weeks wondering where all these needy foster children were. We discovered that the timetable to this service-oriented vocation is rarely one you can anticipate or control. The first call received may not be the best fit for the child or for the foster home. Children who will be readily accepted into one home may have another foster parent wincing with refusal. God knew what He was doing when he made each of us different. He has created a foster parent out there for every foster child; the right fit is the tricky part.

It would be nice if all children who came to live with us in foster care were naturally cute, sweet, and charming, but this is not always the case. Some of these children are a real challenge to care for and enjoy. Not every foster child will immediately be endeared to every member of the family. Over time, fonder feelings will come along. We once had a little girl who had such unusual facial features and expressions that she had the same look whether she was mad, sad, or glad. But underneath all of that she was the greatest kiddo. Reanne had the funniest antics and personality; it just took a little time for us to grow enough in our role to see it.

Our first experience with a single foster child began with a call from the weekend placement worker for a five-year-old little girl named Sarah. We were dressed up and getting ready to head out the door for dinner with coworkers from my husband's office when we received the call. We had to cancel our plans to be home for the caseworker to drop the child off. When the little redheaded girl came in, she was barely two, not five as the worker originally stated. Also, her name was Suzette. Two weeks later we were called again for siblings Amy and Jimmy, and with that our career was off and running.

Once, a placement call came in for a five-year-old little boy, Noah, who had been placed with us the year previous and who had come back into agency custody. This time the call was not only for him but for his brother, Bruce. My husband and I had two small children of our own at the time, and the original boy,

Noah, had been a very busy guy when we previously had him. I remember the initial decision felt like a "no" because it already seemed chaotic enough in our house. After consideration and prayer, I decided to take them both in—mostly for continuity of care for Noah. My husband came home to supper that evening, not knowing about the call for the boys. I introduced him to the new brother and then told Bruce to take Foster Dad down to the playroom to see his brother. Next, I heard a huge shout of "Dad!" and my husband warmly shouted back, "Noah!" They were absolutely overjoyed to see each other again. It was a heartwarming moment and a very busy placement, but it ended up being a great decision. To this day, we keep in touch with these two beloved young men and their families. They will always be family to us, and we are extremely proud to have been their foster parents.

My advice is to help foster parents understand that, when the placement call for a potential foster child comes in, it will not be a calm, quiet time. It will likely come while you are at the grocery store, at work, or during a hectic homework session. I stop what I am doing, find a quiet place to take the call, get out paper and pen, and write down everything that is said. Sometimes there are details given during that first call that I will never hear again. Ages and sexes of the children are readily provided with the placement call along with a brief explanation of the reason for removal and known major medical conditions. However, be aware of the iceberg! Foster parents must understand that they are basing their decision on only known basic details. I am not a big fan of the words *always* or *never*, but in this case, there is always incomplete information given prior to you making the decision to take a stranger into your home.

When I am talking to the placing social worker, there are a few non-negotiable questions that I have learned to ask before hanging up the phone. I inquire about the birth dates of the children. Often, the birth dates are quickly glanced at by the worker, and the ages given are inaccurate. I ask about immediate medical concerns and any major behavior problems that are unusual for the chronological age of the child. A child who wets the bed at age three is a different story than one who wets at fifteen. I ask if the child has any siblings or cousins in foster care. I ask where the child's family is geographically located and about any past issues related to arson, animal abuse, or sexual abuse.

Foster parents take children in with no notice and with little knowledge of what the children's actual needs are or what the expected duration of stay is. The placement timeline needed for a foster child could be two days, two weeks, two months, or two years. We know a foster family who took a child in late at night, and the only information known was a first name, sex, and approximate age of the small child. The next day, when more information came, the first name of the child was wrong, and it was discovered later that the child's last name was completely different from what the agency staff had been told, probably to throw the authorities off.

Most agencies do have an assessment tool that answers questions that give a further history of the child to the foster family. The problem is that this information is usually provided after the family has accepted the child. The assessment tool forms are most often delivered with the child and the intake paperwork when the child shows up at your house. In addition, the forms are often filled out by someone who has little firsthand knowledge of the child. Thus, the responses can be generic and, unfortunately, inaccurate. Recently, our twelve-year-old foster son arrived with his assessment tool that referred to him repeatedly as "the baby": "The baby has a history of fire setting and animal cruelty." "The baby is truant from school," the report read. The placement caller accurately reported his twelve-year-old age to us, however no information on arson or animal abuse had been given. Foster parents have the responsibility to ask good questions in order to protect the children already in the home as well as to protect and care for the child being considered for placement.

One late Friday afternoon I received a call for a six-month-old baby, Anne, who was being discharged from the hospital. I was told she had been born prematurely but was doing well overall. When the child was brought to our house, she was smaller than a normal newborn and barely weighed five pounds! She had only been out of the PICU a few days! She had actually been born a micro-preemie six months previous; her weight at birth was just one pound two ounces, and she was only six inches in length—the same length as a cell phone. She was also severely drug exposed and was still actively going through treatment for withdrawal. The situation presented at my front door on a holiday weekend was an entirely different situation than what was described to me on the phone, what I agreed to, and what I had planned for. Tiny Anne slept in a cradle two inches from my face because I was so worried about her small size and fragile state. Because of this case, and another incident with an exceptionally large teen, I have gotten a lot better at asking questions about the age and size of children before I accept them into our home.

When a placement call comes in, I carefully think about the information and pray for the children facing the trauma of the day. I pray too for the parents whose children have been removed and that good decisions are being made by those in charge. Lastly, I pray that the needs of God's children can be put before my own. Then, I make a return phone call to the agency, and if the placement is the right child at the right time, we accept the child into our home.

When a child first comes to our home, we try not to be overly exuberant or loud. I find that having one person quietly answer the door and then having no more than my immediate family members present sitting casually around the kitchen and family room is least overwhelming. Refraining from having many people run into the child's personal space to exuberantly greet them helps the child feel comfortable, reduces the stress, and keeps them from feeling like their problems are on display. A kind, quiet, and nonchalant greeting goes a long way to making the child feel less afraid. We smile, take the child's developmental age into account, and explain slowly what is happening to them. By offering sincere concern and giving them a chance to catch their breath, we can help them begin to grasp all that has happened. I once had an overwhelmed child collapse in the hug of my arms because of the stress of that intake day.

Further, we take clues from the children as to how they are doing. Are they sobbing, angry, frightened, or happy? We calmly provide a friendly first impression even if it is not returned. We listen to what the new foster child wants to tell us about the events of the day and about themselves or their family. We give them time to get familiar with us and their new foster home. For older children, we try to look them in the eye and extend a hand. This shows that we are welcoming and not afraid to touch them even if they are unkept or appear to be giving a standoffish attitude. The children will often ask the same questions over and over as they assimilate to the new environment.

I have experienced a range of first responses, from a tender hug to ignoring and swearing. I usually start by saying, "I'm sorry about this crazy day today. What can I do to help?" If the child is little, I squat down to their level and explain that we are a helper mommy or daddy and that this is a special helper home called a foster home. I tell the child that we work with the police officers, social workers, and doctors while assuring them that they are welcome and safe. We reiterate that their family knows where they are and that we are going to take very good care of them until their own family can again. It is important for them to understand these basic concepts.

If the child chooses to share their abuse stories with us, we keep our reactions matter of fact. An "oh dear," "I'm sorry," or "that's sad" comment suffices. We just listen; we do not attempt to fix their problems. Additionally, they definitely do not need to tell their story to everyone they meet. For this reason, I call our relatives and friends those first few weeks to warn them to greet the child without drawing attention to any visible signs of abuse or wounds.

Candace came to our house and started pacing back and forth nervously. Her first sentence to me was asking where we kept our weapons and swords. Talk about shock and awe! Another time, a thirteen-year-old boy named Jesse went to the diaper pail and pulled out a dirty diaper and began to walk around the house coveting it. In a third case, Nelson was absolutely not coming through the front door. He did not care that his brothers were already inside eating soup and sandwiches. This was not his home. My responses were tailored to each individual child. I knew not to show any emotion to the teen girl with the sword comment and got the teen boy redirected shooting baskets outside without the diaper. Ron ended up sitting on the front porch chatting and playing race cars with three-year-old Nelson for over an hour before he finally agreed to come in and eat.

Sometimes the children are beside themselves with emotions that range from sadness and confusion to happiness. Since the emotions of that first meeting are unknown, we must be bravely prepared for the unexpected and remain calm with our reactions. Ten-year-old Nellie bounded out of the social worker's car and ran in the front door yelling "Mom! Dad!" even though she had never met us before. As an adult, she is still very friendly and unfortunately still has the same misplaced bonding issues.

Infants will be welcomed differently all together. They need to have quiet and gentle comfort while they adjust to the new surroundings. We like to use soft baby music, dim lighting, and have the dog outside to promote a less-frightening transition for the baby. We take our best guess at determining when the child last ate. If the last feeding is unknown, we start with small feeds of a regular formula. We want to prevent vomiting or overeating by giving small, frequent amounts of feedings at a time until we know the child's eating habits better. I ask the social worker if the child has any allergies, though this information is typically unknown. Trial, error, and careful observation helps me determine my best plan of action.

Several weeks after the call for tiny baby Anne, we received a call for another six-month-old baby girl, Ella Sue. Upon her arrival, we were surprised by how grossly obese she was. These two same-aged babies were shockingly opposite in size, with one very small and one very large for her age. We were told that Ella Sue was routinely left unattended for hours. She was strapped in an infant seat with eight-ounce bottles propped up in her mouth to keep her quiet while the mother went out, leaving her home alone. Basically, it was eat or drown. This situation is very unpleasant to think about. She was slow to warm up to people holding her for feedings and had to have her formula amounts decreased slowly, per doctor's orders. This was another big adjustment beyond being placed in foster care and having a new caretaker. It is hard to imagine what goes through a very young child's mind with all these sudden changes.

We have cared for quite a few babies and toddlers who have spent an excessive amount of time restrained in car seats and playpens. They may easily be frightened, be withdrawn, or may shy away from touch altogether because they have not bonded with their caregivers in the usual way. They have been unable to depend on their cries to bring attention and positive responses. Even the very young have experienced trauma and can show signs of being stunned. We are careful to watch them especially closely for safety issues because they can be physically weak, fall easily, and lack experience with steps, etc. Thankfully, they are resilient and learn to trust and grow with tender loving care.

Once we have our initial hellos behind us, I ask the children if they are hungry. Typically, they have been snacking for hours at the police station, the local child welfare agency, or the school principal's office. I offer them a few choices for a snack until I have a better understanding of their food likes and dislikes. We are fairly lenient in this area because food is a small issue compared to everything else going on. When they arrive late, I say, "I have PB crackers, cheese sticks, and milk. Which ones would you like?" That saves me the entire conversation of saying "No, we are not having candy at 2am." Making them feel comfortable and secure is the goal.

Children will frequently put on a show of antics and attention-seeking behaviors upon arrival into foster care because they are disorientated, scared, or mad. After Candace asked about our weapons, I paused and nonchalantly stated we did not own swords or weapons in our home but that she could talk to me about her swords if she wanted to. Turns out, she had no swords and was just looking for a bigger response from me. When she did not get one, she moved on to another topic and disclosed that she was a good artist. We made a point of going shopping for art supplies even before we went shopping for clothes. This special outing did wonders to break the ice between us because it gave this sullen girl and this "strange new foster mom person" something non-threatening to talk about.

As Elizabeth and I went into the agency to pick up a new set of siblings one afternoon, three-year-old Davey ran around in circles in the busy agency waiting room yelling and acting aggressively. As I got closer, I remember thinking "please, God, don't let that be my child." Of course, he was, and he carried on for quite a while until he was dizzy and finally tired out. The young caseworker watching him was beside herself with his loud energy, and she tried repeatedly to stop him. He was clearly overwhelmed with the unfamiliar events going on around him, and this seemed to be his way of coping. I did not attempt to curb his behavior because it was likely that these antics were the only way he knew how to express his emotions, and frankly, I knew the likelihood of me teaching him proper behavior in public at that exact moment had a low probability of working. That same social worker was pleasantly surprised a few days later when she came to our house for a visit and saw what a delightful little guy was hidden underneath all the insecurity and nervous energy of that first night. We are glad to have gotten to know Davey after all because many years later he, his siblings, and his parents are still cherished friends of ours.

We help children settle into foster care by accentuating their positive behaviors and downplaying the negative ones. Requests are kept simple to understand, especially those first few days. We repeat simple statements about being in foster care, tell them again who we are, and describe what foster care is, reassuring the children that they are safe. We ignore bad behavior choices and cheerfully comment when we see good ones because children enjoy being "caught" making good choices. Setting daily routines makes getting into the swing of our schedule easier for the child to follow. All these small tactics help the children feel more confident that they can get through what being a foster child entails.

After the children have warmed up, I do a cursory assessment of their physical health to better understand what trauma they may have experienced. I follow up with the caseworker to make sure any marks, bruises, and abnormalities have been documented. I ask permission from the caseworker if I may take photos of the abuse to send to them immediately if we discover something that has not been previously documented. I heard once of a foster parent getting reported to authorities by a photo lab for printing pictures of a child with bruises. Situations like these are why immediately notifying the agency staff and documenting any potential abuse marks is of vital importance and will provide proof should questions ever be raised.

Even though children know what their abusers did to them, most will still want to go home. Daniel came to us with a well-defined black and blue handprint across his face. Bryant had a swollen bruised eye and multiple stitches near his eyebrow. Krissy had belt marks across her back. Buck had cigarette burns on his hands and legs and a huge, deep scar that ran the entire length of his arm. Though shocking, severe punishments can seem normal to them. All the children know is they want to be with their parents again where the world is familiar, regardless of the abuse and neglect they may have experienced.

We also immediately tend to any significant medical needs of the child. Twelve-month-old Jeremiah arrived late one evening with extensive crusty and bleeding eczema patches. He had dirty seeping wounds all over his face, legs, and backside. I had never seen such extensive skin irritation. I ended up taking him to the emergency room within an hour of him being placed in our home for this severe and clearly uncomfortable condition. Steroids and antibiotics were needed, and accurate documentation—including pictorial proof of his condition—was done by the hospital staff. He and his siblings were so dirty that we emptied and refilled the bathtub water four times that night before the water ran somewhat clear.

One set of siblings—Laura (six), Steve (five), and Henry (one)—were severely neglected and apparently had been forced to spend a great deal of time in a closet of some sort. When they were finally discovered by the police, a fourth sibling was already deceased in the closet. The siblings' dispositions ranged from out-of-control energy to haunted eyes to an eerie nonverbal daze. The abuse that they suffered must have been horrific. We experienced big emotional swings with them that required our deepest caring and most patient understanding. We knew so little about them because all were nonverbal. My children and I spent a lot of time sitting on the floor in the playroom with them. We watched the six-year-old crawl around on a gym mat, pick up toys, put them in her mouth, and generally explore the environment like a baby would. We used smiles, waves, and slow gentle movements with our hands as a form of communication and never approached them from behind because this seemed to startle them. We certainly could not expect much in the way of rules or structure with these children for quite some time. Medical personnel and therapists had a big job guiding therapy for their shock, trauma, and loss issues.

Stress, chaos, and an unstructured environment are common in most of the homes many foster children come from. Our home encourages a calmer atmosphere, and we do not feed into the out-of-control energy of a foster child. Children notoriously use a loud yelling voice at the child who is only four inches away from them, and many talk to themselves incessantly. Sometimes people jump to the conclusion that children are hyperactive, but we have asked doctors if new foster children coming to live with us can be removed from medication so that we can get to know them unmedicated. Some children will still need medication later, but this gives everyone involved in the child's care time to get to know them first. In the meantime, we work diligently on socially acceptable voices, calm behaviors, respect of personal space, and the setting of routines.

We have seen some level of stress reduction in all children once they realize our home is a safe place and their needs will be met. School-aged children and teens can understand that their parents have not gone away and that there are serious problems that need correction before they can return home. All children, regardless of age, can sense the kindness of a smile, the calm of a stable environment, and of course the feel of ample food in their stomachs. They begin to feel comfortable letting their guard down as they start to understand that they will be well taken care of. We find accepting foster children into our lives to be very rewarding because all children affect us in one way or another.

CHAPTER 12: THE HONEYMOON PERIOD

Foster children and foster parents need time to adjust to each other. The ups and downs of the first few weeks the children are in care are often referred to as the honeymoon period. Our experience has been that older children and younger children have opposite reactions to foster care. In general, we have found that school-aged children and teenagers typically go through the honeymoon period first. This phase of time is initially easier but then, behaviorally, can become more of a challenge. On the other hand, the rationale for foster care is nearly impossible to explain to toddlers and babies, so their honeymoon period seems opposite. They can have a harder time with settling in initially because the changes must be so confusing to them. Once a routine is in place, they eventually adjust well.

In our house, every child is welcomed and gets their own area, including a bed, dresser, closet, shelves, and a small reading lamp. Children can decide when to turn off their individual light when they are ready to sleep, which staves off many bedtime fears. We do not store toys in the bedrooms. Instead, we offer clean, age-appropriate books to be read before bed or when the children wake up early in the morning. Blank notebooks are kept handy for older children if they choose to journal or doodle. We have found that many children have never owned intact books or journals. These interventions are done to help keep the children occupied with quality reading materials rather than distracted with toys. These soothing bedtime practices will, we hope, lead to a steady sleep routine.

We encourage the children to create a cozy space for themselves as a home away from home. A favorite activity is letting them choose a bed linen set and other decorations to personalize their sleeping areas. We have six standard bedroom comforters stored in our linen consignment area. Children and teenagers can choose from several different themed sets: pink ballet, purple unicorns, teal beach, transportation, sports, and camo. We have various pictures and wall art to match, and all children enjoy decorating their area to their liking. We like to think these activities help children feel less out of control because it gives them a space to call their own.

Coloring pages and other art supplies are offered to the children to make room decorations. Conversations about their favorite color, action figure, or book series can be a starting point to get to know them better and help them develop their imaginations. If the children are not interested in crafts per se, they can choose from rolls of children's themed wrapping paper to wrap empty picture frames, creating a fun decoration. Miguel (thirteen years old) especially liked the superheroes gift wrap and used it to cover most of the wall area by his bed. I have yet to have a foster child—young or old, girl or boy—who did not want to personalize their area of the room.

Music seems to be a huge stress reliever when children are new to our home. We often keep music playing in our kitchen area as a soothing tool for children. The music helps with the quiet awkwardness as they adjust. We alternate all kinds of music, so everyone gets to hear the tunes they like. The car dancing that accompanies G-rated rap music is a favorite! Various types of musical toys and play instruments are stashed in every room, and we consistently see those being the chosen toy. The impromptu band parade inevitably comes to life.

We also like to keep a stash of clean, plush, stuffed animals to allow the children to choose from as another comfort measure. All ages from toddlers to teens, even the big boys, love this sentiment. One winter we had three teens already in our care, and then a late-night plea came in for five more children. We were definitely scrounging our stock that night to have enough stuffed animals for the children to snuggle up with.

After physically getting their rooms set up, we start to give simple explanations as to how a foster home runs. We expect a lot from our children, so providing clear, consistent explanations is the only fair way of parenting. Foster children are already forced to accept so much change that they appreciate the rules in foster care remaining simple and steady. Children have more reasons to be agreeable when they feel they are being treated fairly. We all want someone in our corner explaining what is going on in a way we can understand and rooting for us to succeed!

Having to live with different rules on different days, siblings Cheyenne and Miguel told us they acted one way when their mom was sober and another when she was high on drugs. The children were trying to survive, and that meant obeying two different mother personalities, one sober and one not. They revealed that running around the neighborhood unattended was perfectly fine some days, and other days this behavior would make her angry enough to beat them. When their mom was high on drugs and cross with them, she would lock the children in their "bad room." They explained that this was an inner room in the basement with no windows and a lock on the outside. When their mom was sober, she would let them out and wonder why they were in there.

Another thing we do during the honeymoon period is adjust the roles the children play, especially when sibling groups come into care. Older foster children are often very protective of younger siblings. We keep an eye on this habit when they first arrive. We compliment older siblings when they are appropriate with their younger siblings and correct less-desirable actions, such as being too bossy. An older sibling's sense of discipline often comes from the way they have been parented themselves. We can get a good idea of what discipline was like in their own home by the way siblings interact with each other.

The older sibling's discipline style toward their younger siblings can be both good and bad. Realistically, the older child may continue to be the parent figure again if the children go back home, so we aim to teach better habits. We explain that we do not hit in foster care and instead encourage placing two troublemaker siblings into separate play spaces. This is a teachable moment for the older parentified child. Over time though, we want to shift the older sibling's role away from acting like a parent. I let the older child know I sincerely respect the job they have taken on and assure them that there will still be a need for their best big sister or brother care from time to time, but parenting is no longer their primary job. They are encouraged to take more time to concentrate on their own needs and wants. This will validate the good they have done attending to their younger siblings while giving them encouragement to be a child.

The initial intake days are best used to learn about the children and to start to formulate a multifaceted game plan regarding the most urgent needs. Basically, on day two of having the foster children in my home, I start making necessary medical and educational phone calls. I make these calls first because I want to address the children's most immediate needs promptly, and because of the overwhelming numbers of foster children needing services, getting problems evaluated and solved is a time-consuming effort. The needed services will depend on the ages and condition of the children. Scheduling medical and school appointments requires endless patience. I have had to learn to be highly productive while listening to endless phone-loop messages, as most foster children's records are not permitted to be accessed via electronic accounts.

One teen who came to live with us had already missed eighty-eight days of school in the fall/winter term of that school year. Her excuses as to why she did not attend school on a particular day were too numerous to count. We set up conferences with all her teachers the second week she was with us and listened to their suggestions for her success. We encouraged her to care about her daily routine, school schedule, and academic opportunities. In the remaining six months of 8th grade, she missed only two days of school (for strep throat). She went on to make Student of the Month honors by the end of the school year.

We do our best to identify areas of concern early in the placement because it is such a long process to get a need evaluated and treated. Unfortunately, most foster children are notoriously behind in their medical care. I remember one day at the pediatrician's office when our new set of preschool-aged siblings had to have five vaccines each. In addition, they both needed a blood draw and a finger prick to check lead levels. I asked the staff several times if we could split the needle sticks into at least two appointments just to spare the children the trauma of seven sticks in one day. The staff said no because the children's medical benefits would not pay for an additional appointment. It was traumatic for my daughter and me to hold them and witness this; I cannot even imagine what the children thought. We all left the office stunned that day.

If a pediatrician recommends the child be seen by a specialist, I jump on scheduling this appointment right away. Specialists' offices, such as neurodevelopment, dermatology, and psychiatry, notoriously schedule appointments months in advance. A call in September for one child resulted in a developmental assessment "first available" appointment on May 31st of the following year—an eight-month wait! Further, the initial appointment cannot be scheduled until all paperwork from the foster parent, agency staff, schools, and counselors is completed and received by the office staff. If I make these important calls within the first few days of placement and stay on top of getting the paperwork completed and returned in a timely manner, there is a better chance of getting the child seen and the concerns addressed during the time they are in foster care. The time frame a child will be in foster care is never known, so we use every spare minute being proactive in getting their needs met before their world changes again.

Several children in need of eye and dental surgeries received them during their stay in our home. Orthodontic treatment was started on a few children badly in functional need (cosmetic treatment is not a covered service). With our large sibling group of five, every single child needed evaluations for IEPs (Individual Education Plans) for learning difficulties. It literally took a year to get that one task accomplished because there are so many steps in starting the process and seeing it through to completion for each child. On the day the children were returned to their grandmother, the last child's IEP meeting had just successfully finished earlier that morning. These extremely important academic assessments are used to formulate individualized plans for teaching strategies that take the child's strengths and weaknesses into account. Should the child qualify, this documented plan will lead to action that will follow the child no matter which school they are placed in or where they are living for the next several years.

Some level of educational intervention will be needed for almost every foster child, whether it is learning facial expressions and signing for language development in an infant or a formal IEP assessment for a child in school. We want to get educational professionals' eyes on children as soon as possible. Know that if the child qualifies for Early Intervention (an educational program for children under age three) or an IEP (school-aged intervention), initiating these services is one of the most important interventions you can pursue to help the foster child down the road. Foster parents who are dedicated in getting evaluation requests made, assessments done, and follow-through completed are helping the child significantly in furthering their education. Education is a strong safeguard to boosting their quality of life.

Helping foster children have a voice and telling them that you value their opinions continues the process of a smoother transition into foster care. Teaching children to respectfully and courteously make their needs known helps them learn to express their wants in a socially acceptable way. This practice subdues children's needs to be defensive. Child after child has shown positive behaviors when their opinions and ideas were taken seriously. When Miguel thought 9pm was a reasonable time to turn off the video games and start preparing for school the next day and we thought 7pm was more reasonable, we simply compromised at 8pm. We never had another discussion about this because he helped set the mutually agreed upon boundary the first week he was at our house. In fact, at 8pm he would come and say to me, "Foster Mom, it's 8 o'clock. I'm headed to the shower."

Lastly, I would like to emphasize that the initial adjustment period is filled with question after question from the children. We anticipate foster children's needs and concerns as much as possible and repeat information, refraining from using unfamiliar foster-care language, to help children process all the changes happening around them. Children often assume that being in foster care means they are being adopted. We dispel this myth from the beginning and again explain that we are a helper home until their family can take care of them again. If the child is old enough and asks us directly if it is possible that they may get adopted, we try to be appropriately honest with the simple explanation that many people are working diligently to stabilize their family situation, but we will not know the outcome for sure for a long while. We try to build up children's confidence in the foster-care system by reassuring them that we will do everything possible to help them bridge through this experience of being in foster care and assure them there will be lots of fun days along the way.

Through the years, we have received compliments about how politely our children behave. We used to think we just got easy placement calls, but somewhere along the line it occurred to us that children of all ages thrive when they are treated with an enormous amount of respect and sincere kindness. Ron and I feel our life's work is to build up the next generation by helping children in our home become as strong and educated as possible with whatever time we are given with them. Our hope is that every generation we shape with this type of respectful family living will teach their own family the same.

CHAPTER 13: RULES AND SETTLING IN

While some children may never embrace foster care, most can understand why they are not able to currently live with their family. Usually, their emotions will calm after being in a stable environment for a few weeks, which helps them better absorb the concepts of foster care. The newness of "being a foster child" has worn off for both the foster child and the foster family. Now, the real story of not only surviving but thriving through the daily highs and lows of foster care begins.

It is important that foster parents and any other caretakers of the foster children show a united front regarding rules and expectations. Children get away with less mischief and feel more secure when the rules are consistent. If any behaviors or rules need adjustment, discuss the problem between the adults in private then introduce the agreed-upon changes. Ron and I are big believers in having a united front. We have found that having faith in the behind-the-scenes unity plan is very important in keeping the stress of our parenting low and our resolve steady.

We spend a lot of time getting to know our foster children by asking them open-ended questions about their home life and what the structure looked like there. I ask them who watched out for them. By inquiring how the hours of their day were spent, we get some clue, at least with older children, from where their view of rules and expectations derive. Rules that are consistent with our home life are enthusiastically encouraged; ones that are not get ignored, along with an explanation why they will not be used in our home. The more children are included in establishing boundary rules, the better the odds are that they will internalize these guidelines as measures they are willing to follow. The goal is to teach children self-control, not demand it.

Brothers Mike, Dustin, Frank, and Kyle explained that they were truant from school so often because they had no clean clothes and smelled bad. They also said that if one child was sick (this included headaches, stomachaches, and being too tired from staying up late watching movies) none of them went to school for the day. In this circumstance, we worked on teaching the preteens about correctly using the washing machine themselves and taught a daily showering routine. We shared the rationale of proper rest, good nutrition, and the importance of attending school regularly. These boys liked school and said their classes became much easier once they started going daily and were not constantly behind in their assignments. The boys expressed feeling proud of how clean they looked and were less self-conscious about attending school with their peers.

Some foster children are natural rule followers, but many are not. We lay down our ground rules and simply act like we do not know that there is any other way to behave. We portray an air of confidence that the children are already doing a good job of following the rules. We may spotlight examples of their positive behaviors. This might sound something like, "We are really big on kindness here. You seem to be too." Another might be, "We are glad you are here to stay with us for a while. We ask that you be respectful of us, and we'll be respectful of you too." With these statements, the children are starting to build a realistic idea of what is expected of them.

Rules that guide and do not belittle help children heal and grow. Children sense weakness. They know who lets them get away with naughty behavior and who will not tolerate it. Our sly five-year-old Nevada was not above helping herself to her siblings' Pokémon cards without permission. She was clever, sneaky, and did not care at all about someone else's ownership; she simply wanted those cards. Once the stealing was discovered, the infraction was discussed with her. Our family's "no borrowing without permission" policy was reviewed. We did not throw a huge fit because stealing is such a frequent issue with some children, and it can take years to instill a sense of desire to respect others and their things. We have to do our best to follow through with a similar response every time she steals because it happens often. Developing an understanding of right and wrong does not happen with the correction of one incident.

After years of experience with our family, one of our alternative caregivers has shown time and time again that she is keen at catching on to the tall tales our foster children tend to tell. Over the years, they have tried to convince her of all sorts of activities they were supposedly allowed to do. For instance, she told Cheyenne and Miguel "no" to opening a Netflix account in her name so Foster Mom and Foster Dad would not know about it. She chuckled when she told me, "They think I was born yesterday." She got a kick out of the plea more than anything. Well-meaning but inexperienced alternative caregivers, on the other hand, can feel sorry for children in foster care and can be persuaded into giving privileges that are excessive.

One well-intentioned family who helped with our foster children was generous and kind, but unfortunately our foster children took advantage of them with requests for gifts nearly every time the family offered to babysit. Soon the children started misbehaving when we had errands to run because they were expecting purchases each time we went to the store. Instead of gifts at visits with this family, we encouraged our friends to focus their attention on sharing a hobby, such as fishing, cooking, or teaching the game of Chess, which they did. These life experiences help children with thinking skills, with strategy, and with relaxation, and the supervised quality time is a priceless gift.

Our sibling group of five, ages five to ten, was not easy to travel with in a car due to their constant bickering and picking on each other. Amongst other rude habits, burps and belches were nonstop. Consistent correction of their manners eventually showed progress with more polite behavior toward each other. One day, we went to my friend's home for a brief visit, and she met our foster children. This encounter led to her (and her neighbor) wanting to get to know our "very polite" children better. They both eventually signed up to be alternative caregivers, leading to a day of roller skating, a dinner invitation, and a boat ride, all of which allowed the children to see the fruits of their work on following our politeness rules.

We have found that humor helps with rules, and we often poke fun at ourselves and say, "If you're going out of the house to play, please let someone know. We don't want to lose you!" By stating what you are willing to do, or what you are feeling, the comments are nonthreatening and merely informative. We rarely make negative commands like "Don't do that" because they promote negativity, anger, and bad attitudes. We also do not spend a lot of time negotiating. To limit time for defensive responses from the foster children, we state what is expected then move on with whatever is next in our day.

Another rule the adults in our household go by is to change our approach if the child has a look of apprehension, nervousness, or upset on their face or in their body language when we explain a rule. I say this because children come from diverse backgrounds, and what seems appropriate for one four-year-old today may frighten another four-year-old tomorrow. Children perceive situations differently, and the heightened insecurity of being away from their family adds to it. Four-year-old Lamont can be given a consequence of sitting on stairs alone to interrupt negative behavior, while four-year-old Andie is afraid to be out of my eyesight, so this consequence is frightening for her. If a child is looking worried, confused, or scared, we ask ourselves what we can do to modify what we are saying or doing. Having this focus on our parenting style is a self-imposed safeguard to effectively teach lessons in a kind way.

In addition, we explain to new foster children that we expect them to try their hardest to make good decisions. For example, we help them practice pausing and thinking through their choices before they decide to throw a kick at their sister's head. Witnessing adults model good choices as well as being complimented on their positive behaviors is better accepted than always correcting their mistakes. When they want to play video games instead of completing homework, we might say: "I understand, I really would like to sit down and read my book right now too, but I know I have to get my work done before I relax."

Children also notice when or if you ignore the wrongdoings of others. When a driver cuts me off on the road, I have consciously practiced modeling a better reaction than flying off the handle. I have made a habit of saying something along the lines of, "They must have a sick mom at the hospital." On the other hand, we all make mistakes, and when we do make a mistake, we admit it. I might say "I'm sorry I blamed you. I thought you hit your brother, but I can see now that he tripped over the skateboard." We demonstrate following our own rules of treating each other the way we want to be treated ourselves.

Our rules encourage good decision-making over time, so we give the children many age-appropriate choices to practice this. For bedtime, we would say "Time for closing ceremonies everyone! Do you want to read or brush your teeth first?" We would never ask, "Are you ready for bed?" We control the environment to make our lives easier, without compromising the foster child's feelings. We do this by always offering choices that we are willing to live with and never offering a choice we would not allow them to follow through with should it be chosen.

Our little guy Lamont struggled with some of his behavior choices. On one occasion, I told him I could see how hard he was trying to think when I saw him contemplating an explosive response to his sister ruining his train tracks. I asked him if he wanted to move up to the counter or into Mr. Ron's office to play before his anger got the best of him. This moment of prompting and change in environment gave him a boost of encouragement to help him stop, pause, and think about the situation before he acted and threw a punch. He learned that well-thought-out decisions and low-drama behaviors result in lots of positive attention from me.

Honesty is a rule we strive to teach in our home, but it is a tough sell. Honesty is foreign to so many children because they have learned the exact opposite and lie to survive. Most children do not even consider owning up to lies because, historically, that has not brought good results for them. One boy, Oliver (seven), seemed to lie about everything. He suffered extensive physical abuse and told any lie to any person for any reason because his goal was always to please the adult asking the question. His lying was blatantly obvious, which is a very common coping mechanism that a good deal of foster children use. He eventually was adopted into an amazing family, but he still struggles with the honesty issue because wanting to internalize the inherent reward of being an honest person is slow to develop.

Eight-year-old Jabril stole things from time to time. He would rummage through desks and drawers when he had the chance and would help himself to the items he justified as being needed. After stealing, he would often hide. One day, I went searching for him and found him lying silently under his bed poised to deliver me a blow with a 2x4 slat of wood he had pulled down from the box spring. I de-escalated the problem with a statement that he did not need to hide or defend himself because he was caught doing something wrong and to come out and talk with me. He looked immediately relieved. After spending time trying to understand his big reaction to a small incident, we surmised that he panicked and did not know what else to do. He did have a real knack for writing, so we started encouraging this hobby to help keep him occupied. We had him write lists of to-do projects, items to be bought at the store, and "directions" for the family to follow when putting up the Christmas tree. Anything to keep him busy. His feelings seemed to calm when he spent time writing or drawing. After a while, the instances of lying and stealing decreased. One Christmas letter he wrote read, "Dera Foster Mom and Fosters Dad, I loved the Christmas wishe over with you. I wish your famaily a good night. Happy birthdaiy to Jesuse and ant Mearylou. Jesuse Christ for all things you gave me thank you God for puting me end this nices fosters home I love." What a beautiful blessing this misunderstood boy was. His letter is laminated on my desk, and he is still near and dear to my heart.

One evening as I was chatting with a friend named Francis in her driveway, she was contemplating getting in her car to go search the neighborhood for her two missing teens. It was getting dark when her talented skateboarders came gliding nonchalantly into the driveway. She sternly told them that while they may not have exactly broken the "home before dark" rule, they had bent her trust in their ability to monitor their whereabouts independently. Her expectation was that they were old enough to notice that the sun had gone down, and they should have been home sooner. She was not overly dramatic but wanted them to stop and think about what happened. She is a talented, professional parent and knew this thought exercise was enough to stimulate them into thinking about what had occurred and prompt them to make a better decision next time.

When all other explanations for limit setting fail, we have been known to blame the rules of foster care. Three young siblings—Omar, Tiana, and Jeremiah—who were physically abused in their home by a boyfriend of their mother, suffered night terrors reliving the frequent abuse. They would scream out in their sleep about the "monster man" beating them. Beyond just saying that there was no hitting or beating in our house, we also told them these behaviors were against foster-care rules. Blaming the rules was an enhanced explanation their young minds could understand. Omar would ask me every night, "Are you sure the monster man isn't allowed to come here?" Some children literally do think that monsters exist, and unfortunately, like for this little boy, a monster-like person did live in his life. We assured him that the police officers, judge, and we personally would not allow it.

We take great comfort in knowing our foster children have been taught the beginning skills to cooperate with rule following and having respect for another. Most foster children who pass through our house return home, so having the assurance that we gave them chances to learn age-appropriate cooperation and rule following increases our confidence in their safety skills upon returning home. They will likely grow up to be parents one day themselves, so having this mindset might be passed on to their children too.

CHAPTER 14: DISCIPLINE

Discipline comes from the Latin word *discipulus*, which means student. When parents use discipline, it should be to teach, as you would teach a student. Straightforward discipline helps children grow through guidance. Foster children come from such incredibly special circumstances that discipline must be handled with a great deal of care. Foster children are hesitant about discipline because many have known such harshness in their past. Therefore, foster parents must strive to be kind and consistent because children are often expecting something bad to happen for even minor infractions. Children deserve to be exposed to discipline that is designed to teach and not punish or harm.

One specific reason that disciplining foster children can be a challenge is because the children have been brought up in some insane environments. Children cannot be held responsible for their unpredictable behaviors when all they know is an inconsistent environment. This is not to say that good behavior from foster children cannot be expected, because it can. We look at what we think the child has gone through and the behaviors we are seeing, and we decide how to help the child outgrow the bad habits. Changing our mindset sometimes helps too. Being a professional parent means we focus our thinking based on our vast experiences and then decide which action to take. We try hard to consider the child's upbringing and resist snap decisions.

One of our elementary boys, Jamal, pinched another boy at school. He received an in-school suspension for this infraction from the school staff. When I asked him about the incident, he told me that this boy classmate was pinching a girl student on her backside at recess when no adult was watching. The little girl was small and afraid of the classmate who pinched her and would not say what happened. Jamal had protective tendencies because he was the scapegoat child in his home and was used to protecting his younger brothers. He said he did ask the boy to stop several times but that he "couldn't take it anymore." The school was notified of these details, the other boy's desk was moved away from the girl student, and better observation was promised from the playground monitor. The discipline our foster son received did not change because he did pinch the boy; however, we also acknowledged his kindness in watching out for the little girl. Maybe the teacher giving him the "Caring Student" certificate at the end of the school year was partially a result of this experience.

Some foster children become desensitized to harsh discipline. Tragically, many have been beaten whether they followed the rules or not. Children have become confused as to what decision they are supposed to make because their past experiences often include parents who are under the influence of drugs or alcohol. This drugged parenting causes parents to be completely out of touch with what is reasonable, so children have no chance of guessing which rule to follow on which day. Shockingly, household items such as cigarettes, curling irons, and torches to inflict burns are sometimes used as quick discipline tools. Scissors, knives, and bats have left giant scars— both physically and emotionally—on some of our foster children. These "disciplines" do not teach anything but violence and mistrust.

Because children have known uncertainty, especially regarding discipline, we want to be consistent and fair-minded so they can relax and settle into our routine. Our disciplines focus mainly on preventing problems before they start rather than using beginner parenting techniques to react to misbehavior. We steer away from disciplines like time-out and grounding and instead use "time-in," "owe a no," and/or have a "sit-in," which are far more effective types of discipline. As a foster parent, we need to ensure that the punishment fits the crime, is developmentally appropriate, and teaches a lesson.

We rarely use time-outs because they are generally overused and lose their effectiveness quickly. On rare occasions when we do use this discipline, our time-out would center around interrupting the behavior, having the child process what they could have done differently to avoid the negative behavior, and thinking compassionately about the person they offended. Time-outs, when we choose to use them, are kept short because we get bored with them, and we feel that children do also. Besides, more often than not, children will sit in time-out thinking about how much they hate you rather than reflecting on their wrongdoing.

Instead of immediately banishing a child to time-out, we help them understand empathy toward the other child after an infraction. We might say to the one hurt, "I'm sorry you were hit. Are you okay?" We finish the brief interruption of negative behavior with a quick corrective statement to the offending child such as, "If you are kind to Gregory, he will want to come over and play more often" and a compassionate gesture such as a smile to the hurt child. Both children will be asked to "go try again." Thus, within twenty seconds, the issue has been resolved, and we have prevented the need for a time-out. Children who experience this type of consistent discipline will know that they need to correct the behavior or a follow-through with another interruption of their playtime will soon occur.

For children who refuse to alter their behavior after this type of infraction, we may use a short time-out. After thirty seconds, we ask if the child knows why they are sitting there. If they will not answer, then they sit another thirty seconds with a reminder from us again as to why they are sitting there. After one minute of a time-out, the child will either answer as to why they are sitting in time-out, or they will not. If not, we restate what happened, "You are sitting because you were hitting and spitting at Gregory," followed immediately with, "Okay, go try again." If the misbehavior happens again, the environment would then be changed altogether, and the offending child would move to a different activity in a new space. While possibly effective in settings where the child is at a visit or therapy for an hour at a time, time-outs may work, but repeated use of them becomes a power struggle and a tedious task in the 24/7 situation that is foster care.

We also see that time-out is a common discipline technique taught at all community parenting classes. When foster children are at visits with their parents, we try to help the parents decrease the use of endless poorly executed time-outs and instead teach the parents to briefly interrupt the child's infraction and redirect them to another activity. Bringing calm attention to the negative behavior is more helpful than the child saying with exact correctness why they are sitting in time-out. Further, I might encourage good behavior by saying, "I think Jesus would be happy if you allowed your brother to play kickball with you too." If disrupting, distracting, and redirecting are used consistently, time-outs will rarely be needed.

"Time-in" is a far superior discipline tool to time-out. Time-in works by using coaching skills in combination with extra practice time for a child to achieve a skill. Children misbehave for a variety of reasons, such as a lack of preparation, inconsistent rules, confusion, or fatigue. Active parents teach children HOW to act in certain situations. I refer to extra verbal prompting and the practice of appropriate expectations ahead of time as time-in because extra time is needed to teach the child proactively rather than disciplining the child after the infraction has occurred.

For instance, say you need to take your foster child to a school meeting that you routinely attend every month. Last month when you attended, the child constantly interrupted and failed to listen. Try asking the host if you may come to the meeting five minutes early to "practice" good behavior in preparation of the meeting. Explain to the child how you will be there five minutes longer this time because you are needing to take him early so he can practice getting settled and oriented to what is expected of him during an adult meeting. Children are smart. They do not want to go earlier than necessary. After the meeting is over, briefly discuss if the behaviors were more acceptable or not. Adjust the details as needed, but make sure to follow through. Strong parents never threaten an extra time-in session or a time-out discipline without absolute follow-through.

While claiming to like going to church to hear the music, Lexie had not learned how to attend without distracting others with her antsy behaviors of constantly looking around and kicking her legs at the person in front of her. As a result, we had a day where we attended Mass twice to practice. At the first hint of mischief with the first early Mass of the morning, I whispered to Lexie that I was having a hard time listening because she was distracting me. If she chose to continue, we would come back and practice again in an hour at the next Mass. She defiantly said that returning would be fun, so we attended our second Mass of the day. By the end of the second try, we both had a better hour of study and worship. After that "practice Sunday," we enjoyed excellent behavior in church going forward. Lexie had some tough behaviors, but with practice she learned the expectation of being a calm and quiet church participant and that I meant what I said.

We are not big supporters of the grounding discipline either and would rather focus on helping children learn to think before they act, contemplate the choices, make a decision, and live with the consequences of the decision to prevent the need for grounding all together. Most children get good at making age-appropriate choices if they are well prepared, kindly supported, and experience steady follow-through each time. In our home, we let the children remove their own privileges if they make a wrong choice.

Try saying to older children, "If your chores are done by 11am, we can go to lunch at the mall." This statement gives them the opportunity to decide to participate or not. If they do their chores, then all is well. If the child does not, then lunch at the mall would be unceremoniously cancelled, and we would eat peanut butter and jelly at home instead. For littles, instead of threatening to ground them for not doing chores, I matter-of-factly state, "We will get the video games out after the toys are cleaned up and the dog is fed." I enjoy watching how fast the children get their chores done. They know, because follow-through always happens, that the video games will be absent for the day should they choose to ignore their chore detail.

One teen, Dollie, was particularly challenging with her moodiness, negativity, and dishonesty. We were emotionally exhausted trying to be active parents to her argumentative personality. We had to phone a friend and take several days off from being her caregivers once because we were struggling with our patience. Our dear foster friends happily suggested that Dollie could join their family on "team demolition" at their house for those few days. They had spring yard cleanup and gardening to do, wallpaper to tear off the kitchen walls, and painting projects planned. We avoided a grounding situation, removed her from our personal space for a few days, allowed her to learn some home maintenance skills, and remained cheerful with the other children placed with us while on our mini vacation from Dollie. Dollie was not present at our house where she would have likely spent her time being rude and disrespectful. When she came back, she was a transformed girl and cheerfully appreciated her time with us more.

We have all seen the irritated parent threatening the unruly and screaming child in the grocery store checkout line. I once heard a mother threaten a four- or five-year-old child with "being grounded for a week" if they touched the candy on the counter again. I still remember how unrealistic and inappropriate that threat was. Checkout lines are tempting for all of us to want to buy extra treats. The mother needed to teach her child ahead of time that their family does not buy treats at the checkout aisle and calmly follow through each time. Grounding was not age appropriate, nor did it fit the crime of touching a piece of candy. Because I do not think it's an effective punishment, I have no actual grounding examples to give.

The idea to "owe a no" came from the need to train our adult brains to have a quick go-to response when emotions are high or if we are feeling close to losing control. This response works to quickly de-escalate a situation, and once we follow through with this discipline several times it will help a child or teen learn to back down. For example, when a situation has escalated to the point where a teen wants to throw valuable objects across the room, I state, "If you choose to throw that, I will owe you a no." The first time the technique is used it will likely not work. If it is a big infraction, I will immediately owe a big no in response to the child's action, such as loss of a promised fun day at the water park with peers. If it is a small issue, the owed no will be a small consequence. So neither the child nor I forget about the "owed no," I redeem the removal of privilege within a timely manner, usually within twenty-four hours. I follow through no matter what, making the technique very effective.

Candace was large in stature and physically aggressive. She threw items and swore when she was mad, then stomped around the house for hours to make sure everyone remembered how cross she was. When I felt frustrated, I would tell her, "Either get your feelings calmed down and stop pounding around the house or I owe you a no tomorrow when it is time for you to go to the movies." This would usually persuade her to calm down because, like any teen, she wanted to spend time with her friends at the movies.

Owing a no can also be effective if a child does not want to start a task they have been given. I decide on a time frame that I am willing to wait, and then I use the phrase. For example: "I have from 3 till 4pm today to help you sort your summer clothes. After that I will clean your room myself and owe you a no." If I must do the chore, the next time the child asks for a privilege, I remind them that I owed them a "no" from the day when they chose to have me sort clothes in their room instead of doing the task themselves. I think the owe a no discipline is effective because it quickly de-escalates drama and involves no power struggle.

Our school-aged foster daughter Maya enjoyed baking; however, her downfall was that she routinely left the bathroom a complete mess. The owe-a-no technique worked well with her because she did not like losing her kitchen baking privileges. I would comment, "Feel free to start your cupcakes as soon as the bathroom has been tidied." I had to follow through with removing baking privileges a couple of times, but eventually she caught on to the idea. I paired this approach with a comment about how, for now, she was part of our family, and tidying the bathroom after herself was a task that was expected of all family members in our home. She eventually developed a sense of belonging with our family, and the messes became less of an issue. After being reunited with her father, she returned for four consecutive years to visit and bake a birthday cake in preparation for her special day. She told me that she began using this same technique at home with her eight younger brothers and sisters.

Lastly, we like the idea of the "sit-in" discipline. This strategy works like a charm with preteens and teens. All that is needed to accomplish this technique is a few minutes of unwanted adult time and an obnoxiously large stack of paperwork. Let me explain. When I see misbehavior escalating between teens, I literally insert myself into the middle of their behavior before emotions get out of control. Making myself large and in charge right in the middle of the developing drama quickly seems to take the steam out of the confrontation and de-escalates the problem. They typically are not looking to sort out their innermost feelings in front of me and usually move on with a more appropriate activity. On the occasion that the teens do want to talk, then I am all in for good communication to solve a problem.

We were bothered by how poorly Kelly (eight), Kym (seven), and Katie (six) picked on and criticized each other and had little respect for personal space. After repeated requests to curb the behavior, I decided that instead of separating them, I would simply add myself into the behavior by having a sit-in. The only intervention that was needed to disrupt their bickering was for me to sit down on the couch or at the kitchen table near the arguing siblings. I was deep in thought as I methodically went through each and every piece of my paperwork and was in no hurry to leave their presence. Their eye rolling was nearly audible as I silently interrupted their debate. After I resorted to this technique a few times, they learned to automatically stop their bickering as soon as I glanced their way and started gathering my work papers. They came to the realization that their sisters were not so bad after all, and they wanted to spend time doing activities with their peer siblings rather than spending time sitting next to Foster Mom. Desperate times call for desperate measures sometimes. Eventually, they started internalizing the discipline themselves, and less tattling and more bonding resulted.

Effective disciplines are critical to develop, use, and teach. Foster parents can drive themselves crazy with worry about the past, cruel punishments their foster children have endured, so this further drives our desire to create effective and creative disciplines that are kind. There may even be the opportunity to teach some rudimentary steps of these disciplines to the child's family directly during interactions at visitation drop-off or pickup times. That is why we take advantage of even a few minutes to model appropriate discipline. Consistency between the two families is important because each time the foster child experiences a kind discipline it helps heal emotional wounds of their past and gives hope that positive change is happening to their family's discipline practices too.

Little Maurice was an energetic three-year-old child who would climb and jump on the chairs in the reception area while waiting with his parents. As soon as he saw me come in to pick him up, he would get down and come over and tell me excitedly about his visit. Over time, watching the positive behavior of Maurice, the parents figured out that he was expected to stay off the furniture when I was around, and they learned to follow through better regarding his behavior. This small example influenced a change in the parenting technique used for Maurice that would hopefully continue when they reunited. Teaching self-control is always a more effective discipline tactic because the children eventually learn to identify and stop the behavior themselves. Self-regulation is crucial insight they will draw on for the rest of their lives.

We know that each child who walks through our front door is one of God's children regardless of how difficult their behaviors or personality may be. We have fostered some very challenging children, but we continue to seek out and emphasize each child's strengths, downplay their weaknesses, and choose the best disciplines to teach them. We want our children to learn to be responsible for themselves and their actions, thereby alleviating the need for parents to police every situation. Fear and pain do not ever help a child grow; kind discipline that evolves into self-control does. All children need an individualized parenting plan to achieve this. (I like to call this an IPP.)

Every single day I think of St. Teresa of Calcutta, who spent her life doing small acts of kindness toward others and with great love. She is such an inspiration to me because I feel that discipline encompasses that same love. Performing small interventions with a cheerful heart is the type of discipline that can make a positive impact on the life of a child. After all, Mother Teresa said that "peace begins with a smile."[8]

CHAPTER 15: STRATEGIES OF ACTIVE PARENTS

Building a stronger foundation for a child begins with being an "active parent." Active parents want their children to grow, learn, and discover something new every day. Clever parenting strategies help active parents in their attempts to teach children to be accountable for their decisions and to think through situations before they act. This effort promotes positive self-esteem and is rooted in self-discipline. Eventually we want children to take over the responsibility of correcting their behaviors independently.

Active parents talk with their children and explain the world around them. They talk about everything from nursery rhymes and spelling words to independent living skills and faith building. A great deal of energy and time is devoted to being an active parent, as active parenting means actually interacting with the child and refusing to succumb to the temptation of having electronic entertainment raise the child instead. This strategy is hard work, but it is also immensely satisfying to see a responsible child develop. The hard part of foster parenting is choosing to be an active parent for someone else's child whom you did not ignore or neglect but are trying desperately to heal.

As Ron and I take our daily walks, we consistently see the same active parents out in their yards, in any season of the year and in any type of weather, spending quality time with their children. One dad is doing lawn work while his sons use child-sized tools to help. A mom practices baseball with her son. Grandpa down the street has all the neighborhood kids organized in a football game. A few blocks away a teen is being taught how to change the oil in the car, and All-American Dad (as we like to refer to him) sets up his TV in his garage so he can participate in his little girls' tea parties and chalk art while he is watching the big game. We are inspired by the high level of commitment active parents have toward their children.

The opposite of active parents is inactive parents. Inactive parents expect the responsibility of their children growing into responsible adults to fall on someone else. They blame teachers when their children are not smart enough, the nosy neighbor for calling Children's Services, and the authorities if their child gets into trouble with the law. Their general mantra is to look elsewhere for their children's formation, when in reality they need to look inward. Active parents monitor their children, know where they are, who they are with, and what they are doing! We like to invite the neighborhood children over for outdoor play or popcorn and a movie so we can get to know our child's peers and their parents.

Two foster children, JJ and Nadia, had a family case plan that failed. The courts determined that their best shot at a good future was adoption. The dear family who adopted JJ and Nadia consider the extra effort of staying in touch with these children's extended biological family a part of their active individualized parenting plan. Several aunts and uncles of the children remain emotionally attached and enjoy checking in on the children from time to time. Though this is not the easiest road some days, the adoptive parents allow this because they are aware of studies that strongly suggest that letting adopted children have some connection with their biological family supports their mental health and emotional well-being as they age.[9]

Natural consequences are the granddaddy of all strategies that active parents use for discipline. Natural consequences teach children lessons based on consistent follow-through of their choices and actions. When children are faced with a decision, we prepare them for what will likely be expected and answer any questions they may have. We allow the children to make their own decisions—within reason—and give them the opportunity to succeed or fail based on what they decide. If the outcome is positive, they know to make the same good choice the next time. If the outcome is poor based on their choice, a natural consequence will ensue. Negative learning opportunities teach that life goes on regardless. Children taught to be resilient learn to survive and cope in an age-appropriate way. Supporting natural consequences teaches this.

We took a trip to the community center one day, and our twelve-year-old foster son Andrew forgot to put his swim trunks on before leaving the house. As a result of his poor planning, he sat on the bench at the edge of the pool, with his goggles and towel, but no swim trunks. He did not complain about not getting to swim because he knew the first direction given to all the children that day was to get their swimsuits on for the pool and then pack their swim bag. Apparently, he had forgotten. We resisted the fleeting thought of going home to get the forgotten swim attire. There was no drama or emotion. In fact, we did not even talk about it. We ended up having a nice chat sitting on the edge of the pool together while the others swam. The next time we went swimming, Andrew took responsibility to get ready for the pool and even asked his brothers and sisters if they had all remembered to put their swimsuits on. We complimented him on being an organized and responsible leader and had a lot of smiling faces that day when the swimming fun started again and everyone got to participate.

With natural consequences, there is a big learning curve with mastering good decision-making for the child. We help them out in the beginning as they are becoming accustomed to the technique. As the foster children start making small choices competently, we move on. When children fail, we ask them to try again, and we resist the urge to complete difficult tasks for them or to think for them in every tough decision. Overmanaging a child sends them the message that you do not think they can do the task on their own. The correct message we want to send is that all actions result in a reaction, good or bad. We do not rescue them from every mistake and instead discuss alternative actions for the next time the situation arises, again all within reason.

Our six-year-old foster daughter LaToya had been complaining about the color of her gloves. Thinking she would get new gloves when she returned to our foster home, she chewed holes in them while she was away on an overnight respite. The respite foster mother watched the chewing incident happen through her kitchen window and relayed the situation to me. LaToya had been asked to stop chewing her gloves once but did not listen and proceeded to successfully put holes in them. The next day, LaToya innocently showed me the mysterious holes. Without anger, I commented to her that her hands might be chilly at the bus stop the next few days since she now had holes in her gloves. Lucky for her, the weather warmed up soon after. Low drama consequences for poor choices mean simple lessons can be taught with no self-esteem damage to the child.

We did not like LaToya's choice to purposefully ruin her gloves but chose not to punish her. Instead, we let the natural result of her action teach the lesson better than a punishment would. Realistically, keeping our own emotions in check can be challenging while correcting the little ones' behaviors. It is not easy to follow through with every one of these incidents. We try very hard to not get emotional because that decreases the effectiveness of the technique. Because patience is power, timing is everything. Deep breaths and a quick prayer help give us a moment to gather that calm at the time of the infraction. An important part of this strategy is knowing the child learned the natural lesson without them knowing it bothered us.

Another good example of a natural consequence happened when Dollie lost her set of earbuds on the bus. As a result, she had to live with the embarrassment of borrowing her little sister's princess headphones for a mandatory listening assignment at school. When she got angry, we expressed that we felt bad she lost her earbuds and helped her brainstorm what to do about the dilemma. We helped her to think about checking the school lost and found and to ask the bus driver. Still, she owned the problem, and we did not solve it for her. At the teacher's suggestion, Dollie ended up earning credit at the school store with timely completed homework assignments for several weeks and "bought" herself a new pair of earbuds. She took very good care of them after that.

I once watched a mom at the store tell her daughter, "I am so sick of always having to tell you things five times before you do what you're told." The problem here is with the parent, not the child. I wanted to teach the mom to follow through by stating quietly and politely one time what she wanted her child to do. If the child ignored her, then she should move up a level to a statement such as, "If you choose to ignore me again by not picking the purse up off the floor, then we will put both the purse and the new shoes back." If the child picked up the purse, the mom could respond with a good job nod and smile. If she did not, then the mother should pick up the purse and shoes and unemotionally put them back with no further conversation about it. Pretend the cries are silent, should they occur, and keep on shopping. If the mom would learn the follow-through concept every time she spoke to her daughter, the child would learn the listening concept, and the mother would no longer be exasperated with her child. I feel genuinely sad to see families struggle with these easily solvable issues.

Redirection is another strategy that active parents use. Redirection utilizes diversion and refocusing before behaviors get out of control. Most of the time, children are striving to build good habits but will need some navigation with their choices. When eleven-year-old Avery starts becoming emotional because her strong personality and sassiness are overwhelming playtime with the other children and tempers are starting to flare, I redirect her by requesting her presence in the kitchen to help me make snacks. This way her behaviors can be discussed and corrected away from the ears of the others. She will be asked to choose between including all the children in the clubhouse play or having the playdate cut short. I will follow through with what she decides. Children learn to appreciate calm intervention before their emotions become too much for them to handle on their own.

If a child is being actively monitored, it should be easy to recognize their individual signs of behavioral wilting before they get overly frustrated, act out, and need discipline. Lamont had many disruptive behaviors, but he was also a good helper. He would frequently pick fights with another youngster when he was losing his self-control. Upon seeing him start to get irritated, we move in to change the scene. We might simply prompt him by saying, "The kitchen trash is overflowing, Lamont." Because he had a helpful nature about him, he would usually stop what he was doing and come into the kitchen to empty the bag. This action prompted comments about how strong and capable he was to be able to pull the bag out, put it in the garage, and replace a clean bag back in the container. He took pride in his ability to help Foster Mommy "all by myself." By this time the frustration in the other room has long passed. Lamont gave many professionals a hard time at school and in counseling, but I think they concentrated on his negative behaviors too much and not his positives. He liked being "caught" being good; he just needed attentive redirection before he lost control. I can see genuine delight in a child's face when they realize they can make their needs known before needing to act out to receive attention.

Another of our favorite parenting strategies is known as the "brain-drain" technique. Children use this on adults all the time. Obviously, children will disagree with what is asked of them from time to time. Children would prefer that parents justify their answers by repeatedly asking the same thing; this drains our (the parents') brains. Children can whine, cry, or barter in response to what is being asked. I have heard, "C'mon, the other kids are going," or "Why not?" or "You're not my mom." The brain-drain parenting strategy allows children's antics to be easily combated by turning the idea around.[10]

Picking one sentence and repeating it back in a respectful and nonemotional manner is the easiest way to do this. "We will head out to the ball field once the sweeping is done." The child might reply, "Our mom doesn't make us sweep at home," or "You get paid to clean." My calm reply would be, "We will head out to the ball field once the sweeping is done." We do not engage in the child's comments, emotions, or attitudes in their attempts to brain drain us, and we do not give in or change our original request. Instead, we use our one chosen sentence and wait patiently until the sweeping is completed.

Another useful parenting strategy is what we call the "cooperation station." This intervention is used when children have difficulty playing together well. Some children are constantly antagonizing each other, and every small infraction is met with a bloodcurdling scream. To curb this behavior, we use station time where we separate the children into different play spaces or stations until they become better at cooperative peer play. While one child plays on the floor with the building set, one is in the highchair with playdough, and another is on the swing in the playroom. We set up different activities and then rotate turns through each. Next, we let them try to play together on their own for short periods of time. If the poor behavior returns, station time begins again. Sometimes the separation and gathering attempt goes on for days. The need for adults to prompt tolerable play will decrease as the children get used to managing play on their own. The arts of cooperative play and dispute resolution are beginner social skills that evolve into positive relationships in other aspects of the child's life.

To further promote cooperation in our foster home, we allow our foster children a "no-thank-you list." This is a short list of approximately five items that they do not want to eat or do. The goal is to make life easier on all members of the family and decrease any trauma that we have control over. We try hard to honor these requests.

Katie strongly disliked all soups and never wanted it near her. Apparently, her family ate canned soup almost every day when food was available at her home. She seemed to associate soup with unpleasant times, so the no-soup request was readily granted. Four-year-old Tre did not have the focus to clean and organize toys. He wound up playing instead and then became frustrated that he never seemed to finish the job. Though he was not permitted to purposefully make large messes for others to clean, he was allowed to add toy organizing to his no-thank-you list. He did, however, like to use the sweeper. His sister Gabby felt the opposite, as she was a master toy organizer but never ever wanted to sweep. Thankfully, we all have our gifts.

Manipulating the environment in our home helps us meet the special needs of our foster children. We have found this helps us keep our foster children monitored and extra safe during their time with us. We do not advertise to the children that we are creating a safe and public space for them to play in but nonchalantly set up boundaries to meet the critical needs of the children without compromising their fun. We use several activity areas in near proximity to the kitchen as play spaces. This is on purpose because the adults in our home spend a great deal of time in this high-traffic area. To ward off as many unwanted behaviors as possible, we want to keep the children within our direct view.

For us, taking in multiple foster children near the same age group helps life go more smoothly, especially when it comes to our designated play areas. We have also been able to take in several unrelated sibling groups at the same time because their ages were similar. This strategy helps with having safe age-appropriate play areas. Examples would be groupings of children where ages were 1,2,3; 2,2,3,4; 2,2,2; and 9,10,11,11,12,12,13,13. We recently had twins who were eighteen months old, so we cordoned off the sunroom and kitchen areas with baby gates to essentially make a giant two-room playpen. This setup allowed a safe and fun play space for the toddler-sized jungle gym along with many gross motor push toys. The twins were safely in our direct line of vision, and they had many age-appropriate activities to choose from.

The summer COVID hit, we had eight foster children ages nine to thirteen. Placements of all older children helped us make the decision to get a small, above-ground pool set up outside the kitchen window. I would not have considered a pool with toddlers in the house, but since all the children were about the same developmentally and were comfortable in the water, this was an excellent time-guzzling summer activity. The children played mermaids, Olympics, synchronized swimming, and spent many fun hours burning off pent-up energy. We think having age-appropriate safety zones increases the fun for the children and decreases the stress for us.

Lastly, as active parents we want to build self-esteem in our foster children. One of the main ways we do this is with the making of memory books. In the foster-care world, these are called Lifebooks because they tell the story of the foster child's life and give an accurate accounting of how their time in foster care was spent. This scrapbook of sorts also serves as a timeline history book and a source of information for the child and their family.

The Lifebook documentation starts when a family team meeting is set up by the agency staff. This important meeting is used to gather pertinent information about the child. After the meeting is completed, I ask to take a family picture for the child's Lifebook. I explain briefly to the foster child's family what a Lifebook or memory book is, why we make one, and that a family photo would be a nice start to the child's Lifebook, if they are agreeable to having one taken. Surprisingly, no parent has ever refused my request to take the photo, and I have been told on more than one occasion that this is the first time a full family picture—with both parents and all the children—has ever been taken.

One mom's answer to my picture request was that she would be in the photo but that the father of her child had never allowed pictures of himself to be taken. The dad looked at me, nodded once, and surprisingly agreed to one photo. He is now incarcerated for life, and this is the one photo the child has of herself with both of her parents together. In another instance, the mom of our foster baby overdosed on drugs and died a few months after the family team meeting. This family photo ended up being a profoundly important piece of history for the child.

As days, weeks, months, and sometimes years go on, we include photos of special outings in the child's Lifebook. Additionally, medical summary notes from doctor visits, school assessments, and a few arts and crafts pages are included. All papers are preserved in chronological order.

Years ago, we had a set of brothers for whom we made some of our first Lifebooks. After the parents' case plan failed, the children left our home and were adopted. We met up with them years later, and they told us how much those Lifebooks meant to them. They explained that they grew up with their Lifebooks displayed on their nightstands. Their adoptive mom would occasionally add photos through the years too. From then on, we would visit them every year or two, snap a photo to commemorate the day, and send the boys each a copy to add into their Lifebooks. They tell us, twenty-five years later, that they still cherish those books, and we assure them that we still completely cherish them too.

In baby Jessa's case, both parents attended the initial family team meeting shortly after she came to our home. After the paperwork for the family's medical history and case-plan objectives were completed, the parents left the meeting and never came back. Ever. The notes and family photo from this meeting were literally the bulk of the information the adoptive family got from us for this little one when she was adopted. The Lifebook might not have been as much in depth as we would have liked, but the family was very grateful to have every bit of information in it.

Foster children absolutely cherish these memory books! Ron and I complete each Lifebook with a personalized "graduation from foster care" letter. This heartfelt sentiment is written to the children as we wish them well on the next leg of their personal journey when the time comes for them to leave us. We tell them how much they meant to us and that they will be remembered, loved, and prayed for forever. That last page is usually filled with tears and kisses. Surely the children know what we mean when we say that, once you are in a foster parent's heart, you are there forever.

Active parents stick together and support each other's efforts because we are all trying to find ingenious and agreeable solutions to problems that arise. Successful parenting is not about being better than anyone else but about learning, growing, and evolving in parenting skills such as natural consequences, redirection, and manipulation of the home environment all in the hopes of raising responsible and safe children. We offer choices and consequences dozens of times a day to train children in self-control. Every well-thought-out choice is a step in building a cheerful, confident child who has a strong foundation. These strategies help them learn to turn away from bad choices and repeat positive ones instead.

CHAPTER 16: ABUSE, NEGLECT, AND DEPENDENCY

Abuse is a physically, sexually, or emotionally harmful act that is intentionally done to a child. Neglect is a purposeful act of omission that causes harm by depriving a child of physical or medical care; environmental, educational, or emotional needs; and/or adequate supervision.[11] Dependency differs from neglect legally because it is found to be inadequate care through no fault of the caregiver, such as a case involving mental illness.[12]

The longer Ron and I are foster parents, the better we understand the long-term implications that abuse and neglect have on children. Within the walls of our home, we want to care for and protect our foster children in any way we can. There are days we are disgusted with the details of the hardships our foster children have endured, and it takes a significant emotional toll on us. Our faith is what keeps us going in our desire to be foster parents. We have learned a lot from the foster children who have come through our home and how they have mightily dealt with issues of abuse and neglect. While we are always looking for paths to help them recover, we are also inspired by their example. This helps us stay strong for them.

We have learned that we must push negative incidents to the back burner and not focus on the details of the child's abuse and neglect but on the needs of the child. We resist dwelling on the children's bandaged arms, blackened eyes, and stitched-up heads. This allows the foster child to make new acquaintances without having to explain to virtual strangers what abuse they suffered. True, the seriousness of the abuse and neglect sometimes makes us wonder if the children should ever go home, but our job is to concentrate on caring for the child, document any concerns carefully, and pray that good decisions are being made by those in charge of the case.

One particularly gruesome case had parents going to jail for nearly beating a child to death. At the last minute, a court of appeals decision resulted in the charges being dismissed without any further punishment. The child's severe head and neck injuries left him to heal in intensive care. His pain, fear, and suffering did not "get dismissed." However, we know that if we want to be involved with foster children, we must work around the uncertainty of the child's case even if we sometimes flat-out disagree with the decisions being made. We continue to provide foster care despite these difficult circumstances because the children deserve kind people to help them survive abuse and neglect regardless of the decisions that are out of our control.

Court-ordered parenting classes are designed to lessen instances of abuse and neglect by teaching families of foster children basic skills to use with their children when they return home. In my opinion, I have not found the acceptance and recall of what is learned in community parenting class to be strong. The theory is good but not useful without extensive and monitored practice sessions with their children. Ron and I feel foster parents need to be highly knowledgeable caregivers who are then willing to turn around and teach the families of the children how to use these parenting techniques. We use every small interaction we have together as a teachable moment. Foster parents willing to work directly with families of foster children, even to a small degree, help fill the gap between book learning and real-life experience.

Willing foster parents use quick, teachable moments to reinforce the lessons the parents have learned in parenting classes. Opportunities to teach may include a few minutes before or after a visit, suggestions relayed through text messages, or discouraging inappropriate conversation on phone-call visits with their children. On occasion, and with the agency's permission, we invite the families to our house. Abusive, neglectful, or inexperienced parents need good parenting skills modeled and demonstrated to them repeatedly when their children are physically present. Many foster children will be going home to the same environment they came from, and the small lessons taught can help mitigate abuse and neglect in the future.

This seems like a good time to state that not all foster children are in foster care because their families are abusive or neglectful. One night a set of teens came into foster care because, while traveling across country, their car was involved in an accident. The children had minor injuries, but the mother had a crushed pelvis and a broken leg. Since her husband was deployed with the military, she was a single parent, and her family was a thousand miles away and unwilling to accept the children as a kinship placement. Her children were taken into foster care for a couple of months until her husband could be discharged from his deployment. This gave her the time to heal sufficiently not only in the hospital but during her stay at the rehabilitation center too.

Observing signs and symptoms of abuse and neglect are small mysteries that active parents work to unravel. A significant role of the foster parent is being a detective. Children do not come with instructions outlining all their various needs, so literally observing the children and figuring out what those concerns are is a big job. The dedication level of the child's foster parent in alleviating pain and suffering for the child cannot be overemphasized.

One foster mom had a little boy who was pleasant most of the time, but every time he got near his snuggle blanket from his previous home, he mysteriously became agitated. The foster mom had washed the blanket but still this seemed to be the trigger. Eventually, the pediatrician, who knew of the biological mom's medical history, was able to shed light on what was happening. He told the foster mom to throw the blanket away because the illicit drug of choice, meth, being used by the child's mother produced residue that did not wash out of clothes or linens. Apparently, the drug residue left behind was the reason the blanket triggered this screaming reaction in the small boy. The foster mom replaced the blanket, and the agitation went away.

Most prevalent today in our society is the neglect so many children suffer because of drug abuse in the family. Normally developed newborns are hard enough to care for with their almost constant needs. Add in nervous system exaggeration and irritability, and drug-exposed babies become even more difficult to care for, and less easy to console. These babies are often born prematurely because of lack of prenatal care and/or exposure to drug or alcohol toxins in the womb during pregnancy. We have seen premature babies suffer from low birth weight, poor muscle tone, immature lungs, oxygen deprivation, vision loss, hearing loss, and a delayed ability to eat by mouth. We have received babies into our care because the child's increased needs are not met by the drug-impaired parents, which results in even more abuse or neglect.

Typical behaviors we have seen in drug-exposed newborns have included abnormal levels of high-pitched screaming alternating with drowsiness—side effects from withdrawal medications. We see these tiny babies suffer jitteriness in their hands and arms and tightness in their legs. They yawn, hiccup, and sneeze often. They can have persistent diarrhea and terrible breakdown of their skin as a result. (Here's a helpful tip: For better comfort, always rinse disposable baby wipes out with warm water before using on broken-down skin areas, even if the wipes are advertised as the sensitive type. I have noticed this seems to cause less crying and faster healing of excoriated skin.) Many of these babies have difficulty gaining weight because they fall asleep while eating and can have a weak suck. Generally weakened muscle tone is common, as are long-term developmental, cognitive, and social problems as they age. A few have had heart and lung defects. Our sweet Jessa suffered withdrawal symptoms for six long months. Attempting to work with the families of these babies has not always been an option for us due to active drug use, incarceration, or overdose deaths. The infant drug exposure cases we have been involved in have not gone well, and in the end the children did not go home.

Physical abuse comes in all forms of injuries from fingernails growing so long that they curl around and back into the child's skin, to inflicted injuries such as skull fractures, and sadly even death. Tragically, we have cared for three sets of siblings who had a sibling die of abuse in their home before the remaining siblings were taken into foster care. Other physical abuses we have cared for range from burns and blunt trauma wounds to lifelong injuries like brain damage. We have fostered children with untreated fractures of the arms, legs, and ribs where medical attention was never sought, and the injuries healed on their own. Some healed in the correct position, and some did not. These injuries are often left untreated, as parents do not want the abuse documented by hospital staff and then used against them.

Some babies and children do not cry for attention when they have a need, likely because they have learned that no positive response will result. It is a very odd phenomenon to see. Other children do not make pain known to caretakers because they are used to chronic pain such as earaches, toothaches, and stomachaches. I have been repulsed at the terrible smell coming from small mouths full of decayed, disintegrated teeth in children as young as a year old. Teens have disclosed enduring whippings and beatings as everyday occurrences. Again, some children think this type of distress is normal.

Our young foster son Omar adjusted to life in our home with ease. He was just a normal child who enjoyed playing sports outside with Matthew and Mr. Ron and was cheerful to be around. A few days into placement, I noticed a dark and deep scar on the underside of his arm. When I asked him about the mark, he told me that he had been intentionally burned with an iron. Preteen Timmy had a similar scar on his leg that was startlingly big and long. He said that was from the day his "leg was almost cut off with a piece of glass." I was sickened to hear of this abuse and found it interesting that neither had previously offered any information about the injuries. It seemed they had become desensitized to the physical abuse faced in their respective homes.

One family told us that the two youngest children, Jada and Josie, were trapped in a hideaway couch bed in an upside-down position and could not get out. Jada explained the feeling of not being able to breathe and being scared. Both children were freed by their older siblings, Dominic and Vincent, but Josie was unresponsive. The children yelled to their sleeping parents for help. The parents first beat Vincent and threw him down the basement stairs because they were furious. Then apparently the parents placed Josie in cold water because they saw that work on TV. Josie did revive but suffered a traumatic brain injury and is still working to overcome her injuries today.

Sexual abuse is hard to comprehend. We learned early on that some children have been forced to both watch and actively participate in these heinous activities. We had a foster daughter whose mother prostitutes for a living. The mother explained that she could charge extra money if her daughter participated in performing sex acts along with her—and she did so ten, fifteen, sometimes twenty times a day. We have been told about children being forced to watch pornography as part of this practice too. These children immediately need excellent, experienced medical care and counseling. The sexually abused and trafficked children we have known about unbelievably range in age from babies to teens, and they always need an extra-big dose of compassionate understanding and tender loving care.

Fostering sexually abused children in our home requires heightened planning. Safety precautions include being extra cautious where the child is playing and with whom. Our communication and explanations to the foster children are concise and clear, and we answer all questions to quell their typical distrust and nervous tendencies. Informing about acceptable boundaries—such as enforcing "G-rated" play, media, language, clothing, and behaviors—reflects this heightened planning. Due to the nature of sexual abuse, I will not share specific stories except to say that the experience of taking a six-month-old infant in for a female exam left me stunned and repulsed.

Emotional abuse, on the other hand, is not as easy to identify as physical abuse but is almost always present. Children who suffer emotional abuse endure being put down, disrespected, and degraded by belittling and yelling. Emotionally abused children talk about being threatened with guns and knives and being blamed for the family's problems. Some of the children we have cared for have been diagnosed with disorders such as attention deficit disorder, attention deficit hyperactivity disorder, obsessive compulsive disorder, depression, anxiety, and suicidal ideation that comes from withstanding long-term abuse and neglect. Emotional abuse steals the child's joy and has many lasting effects.

Parents who are indifferent toward their children altogether are also guilty of emotional abuse. Sometimes the children bear the heavy weight of being reminders of people their families wished to forget. Sixteen-year-old Donna had profound self-esteem issues and was a very sad teen. She once told me, "My mom hated my dad, and she hates me too. She never wanted a kid." It is hard to imagine her going through all the routine stresses of teen life and feeling like no one valued her. She and many other children are told they should have never been born.

Dakota and Brantley told us they were blamed for their parents separating, their mom losing her job, their aunt being killed, their uncle committing suicide, and their dad abandoning them all. Supposedly, they were the "reason" their family fell apart. Another set of siblings said their parents repeatedly threatened to drop them off at the agency to be adopted whenever they got mad at them. No wonder they were so anxious the day they came to our house. They thought they had actually been adopted and would be living with us forever.

Children also frequently come into foster care because of neglect or acts of omission. Neglect comes in various forms. Lack of shelter and food are commonplace for foster children. Lack of shelter often takes the form of "couch hopping," where families stay at relatives' or friends' houses for a period of time but do not have their own place to live. We have had several families who lived in cars, vans, or in and out of homeless shelters. Children's self-esteem takes a hit because most children know that living under a bridge or in a cardboard box is not a typical home. Children in these circumstances are exposed to discomforts like inclement weather conditions, filth, wildlife, and a lack of sanitation and safety. They witness all kinds of adult activities that they should not.

Sleeping in a shipping container, in a park, or on the neighbor's porch swing after darkness sets in is not unheard of. Numerous children have come to us from battered women's shelters where attempts have been made to keep them in the custody of their parents, yet adding this housing support does not always increase the family's chances of staying together. One boy told us his mom kept using "bad drugs" so she would get caught by the police. He said his mom told him that at least she gets "three hots and a cot" while in jail. From my point of view, it seems that many of these cases end up in permanent custody and eventual adoption because the support services for the case are about as high as they can go. When parenting goals cannot be met in this protected setting, it is often not strong enough to also withstand the stresses of the outside world.

Environmental neglect can include filthy living conditions such as overflowing garbage and nonworking toilets. Not securing drugs, alcohol, and medication is also considered environmental neglect. One of our cases had the social worker declaring our foster children's apartment was one of the worst she had ever seen, with rotten food and trash piled high over the floors, documenting "not fit for animal inhabitants much less children." In another case, a five-year-old was found in a basement of a known drug house eating cat excrement due to lack of food and supervision. The police reported his lice infestation was visible on his head from several feet away.

Lack of food is also a big issue of neglect. Four siblings told us there was a severe lack of food at home and they were always hungry. Often, the five- and six-year-old children would sneak to the kitchen at night to make scrambled eggs for their one- and two-year-old siblings because they were so hungry. They were horribly emaciated when they got to our house and all near the zero percentile of growth—a measure that doctors use to track normal height and weight of peer-aged children. In addition, they were classified as failure to thrive, low weight, had terrible eyesight, and had many developmental delays. They told us their large family would split one pack of hot dogs for supper and that the hot dogs had to be stored in a cooler and cooked on the grill because of a lack of working appliances. To survive, the children developed a close relationship with the lunch staff at their school. These kind people filled their book bags with extra snacks to tide them over until they came back to school the next time. Unfortunately, this plan was not always helpful because the kids' parents did not allow them to attend school regularly out of fear the neglect would be discovered.

Another group of siblings told us they had a hard time eating because they had trouble swallowing. The pediatrician said their swallowing difficulties occurred because their throat muscles were extremely weak from lack of textured and solid food consumption. Their weakened throat muscles also explained why their voices were so soft when they spoke. They fought stomach pains, nausea, and gagging from eating. We found that giving small, frequent meals was more comfortable for them those first few months until they started eating better-sized meals and gaining weight. When they were returned home (incredulously) a year later, they had all improved to at least the tenth percentile on the growth chart, showing they were on the road to recovery, at least physically.

Dakota and Brantley shared stories of eating dog food as a meal one day and then saving their last few bites of hamburger to feed a stray cat they had befriended. These children were protective of this neighborhood cat and worried about its well-being every day they were at our house. To put the children's anxious feelings at ease, we had to ask the caseworker to go to the house to see if the cat was still hidden in the children's bedroom. The caseworker reported back that the house was now abandoned but a window had been broken out in their bedroom, so the cat had likely been able to get out. This was another unexpected loss for the children, and they continued to be concerned about the cat's safety and whereabouts, but they did not mention that house or their parents again.

Most children coming into foster care suffer several types of neglect, and almost always medical neglect is one. Chronic medical conditions are often missed or ignored, and immunizations are frequently behind. Six-month-old baby Tony was taken to the emergency room, and his mom reported to the nurse that the baby carrier he was strapped into fell off the kitchen counter. As a skull fracture was confirmed, the staff at the ER called in children's services to investigate. Later that evening, after being placed in foster care, Tony continued to cry inconsolably, so he was taken back to the hospital a second time and was found to also have a fractured arm and several broken ribs. During this deeper investigation, Tony was also discovered to have a chronic condition called sickle cell anemia. This was just the beginning story for our foster friends and their long medical journey with Tony.

Children who chronically miss school suffer from educational neglect. I expected to see children and teens who skipped school, but I was not aware that many children are absent from school because their families will not allow them to go. Children give a variety of reasons, such as they had a bruise or other injury on a body part that showed, or they had no clean clothes, or "our dad makes us watch bad movies with him late at night, so we had to sleep during school time." One set of siblings told us they smelled so bad that they just could not go to school. We have fostered some amazingly savvy foster children who only needed the opportunity to have a fair chance attending school to achieve many successes. As twelve-year-old Kathy told me, "School is actually pretty easy when you go every day." Eight-year-old Kelly went from mostly Ds to As and Bs in three months' time happily attending every school day. They wanted to go to school and learn!

Abandonment by a parent happens when a certain amount of time has passed, as defined by the court in jurisdiction, without parental care or support of the child. On several different occasions, an abandoned baby was placed in our home straight from the hospital because the parents never went back for them after birth. Other abandonment cases involving school-aged children happened when the parent marched their children into the county's child services agency and announced they were never coming back. These children were all eventually adopted. As a result of increasing incidents of abandonment, many states are looking at raising the age a child can be left at a safe location, like a hospital or fire station, without the parents of the child being charged with abandonment.

Lack of supervision is also considered neglectful. It can include not having a babysitter to stay with the children while the parents work and/or repeatedly leaving the children unattended for non-work-related reasons. Parents state that finding a sitter, especially if they work the night shift, can be difficult. Other times, children are left alone while their parents are away engaging in less-noble activities such as prostitution, illegal drug activity, gambling, or drinking. Children tell us how frightened they are to be left alone. They often tell us that they raise each other the best they can. Before Tre and Gabby were placed in foster care, it was reported to me that two-year-old Tre comforted little sister Gabby by patting her back when they were home alone and scared. Three-year-old Tianna threw crackers into the crib of one-year-old Jeremiah because he was hungry and "Mommy had been gone a really long time."

We quickly developed concerns about lack of supervision with another set of siblings when five-year-old Lexie told us she hated light beer and so did her mama. She said, "My mama don't like that light beer, but she do like iced beer. So do Rachel. She put that into Rachel bottle so she sleep good." These facts were all reported to the proper authorities, and yet the children still went home. People who care well for children know there is no excuse good enough to expose children to these dark activities, which honestly, still happens all the time.

Lastly, we wholeheartedly support our foster children's family members who are faithfully attending mental health counseling and sincerely working on other positive changes in their lifestyle to correct their dependency issues. Dependency is the third category still recognized by some as a reason for removing children from their home. In our experience, though, the percentage of true dependency cases is fewer than documented due to times when a dependency (neglect through no fault of the parents) plea is documented because the child welfare officials do not think they can get an abuse or neglect charge to hold up in court.

All adults in our society have the responsibility of being an extra set of eyes and ears for innocent and helpless children. For instance, on occasion, you may be put in the position of needing to notify the authorities of any abuse or neglect you witness. You may see a baby sitting in the front seat of a car in an adult's lap, obviously not restrained in a car seat. You might witness a toddler being dragged into the store bathroom by an exasperated parent because the child was fussy and had to go potty while in the checkout line. You then hear the parent beat the toddler in the bathroom stall all while not letting them go to the bathroom because they were already late getting home. I personally witnessed these events, and as a foster parent and mandated reporter, since I saw something significant, I had to say something to authorities. The airbag might have deployed on the infant in the front seat, and the toddler probably had a potty accident in the car on the way home, leading to an escalating situation. Thankfully, the police were not far behind in either of these situations.

Removing children from their parents is traumatic; however, we have had numerous families of foster children acknowledge that the courts removing their children from their custody, and thereby forcing them to face their failures, was a necessary change for them. The shock of losing their children, usually temporarily, was the jump start they needed to improve their lives. We wish parents could come to this realization before their children had to experience abuse, neglect, and removal.

For other parents, the desire to overcome abuse, neglect, and dependency issues and achieve stability is a long time coming, if ever. Foster children look to us to give them confidence that the system can work because they are nervous and afraid for the loss of their family. We teach that the child welfare system is designed for foster parents to be a bridge in helping them heal and grow while their parents are getting back on track. We encourage the children to settle into a routine with our family until the time comes that their parents can complete their case-plan goals and reunification can be achieved. We tell them we are rooting for their family to succeed.

Working tirelessly to support children and building them up physically and emotionally helps them recover from the past trauma of their young lives and makes them stronger for the future. We want the families of our foster children to have used the time their children were in foster care to sincerely improve their parenting abilities and home environments by meeting the goals of their case plan, including the cessation of anything that will lead to further incidents of abuse and neglect. We hope that our foster children have learned enough in the time they were with us to make a significant difference in the quality of their fragile lives.

We also must acknowledge that we will rarely know the end of the child's story, so praying for protection from future abuses and neglect is a prayer we repeat over and over, with child after child. I am often heard saying that the foster children came to us with one hundred problems, and we were able to help with seventy. The hardest part of being a foster parent is never really knowing if enough was ENOUGH.

CHAPTER 17: COMMUNICATION AND DEVELOPMENTAL DELAYS

Foster parents attempt to strengthen children, families, and ultimately, communities by the work they do every day. Unfortunately, communication and developmental delays of all kinds are commonplace in the foster-care world. Varying degrees of delays are found to affect foster children, and in many cases, their family members as well. While numerous categories of delays exist, I will focus mostly on delays in communication, including speech and language, and physical delays, including gross and fine motor. Because these delays are such a big part of many foster children's lives, it is vital that foster parents get them diagnosed and treated. Doing so helps more people understand what is going on with these children. It is also important for community members to understand how profound the effects of delays are, sometimes affecting every aspect of the individual's life.

Communication delays are manifested in speech and language issues. They are prevalent for many reasons, including a lack of verbal stimulation. Over the years, numerous doctors have expressed concern about the correlation between parental distraction and a child's delay with verbal skills. Though extremely necessary, eye contact is rare in many homes. Speech therapists are constantly preaching the benefit of putting down the cell phones and talking, reading, and singing to children, but a lot of parents fail to realize that a lack of verbal skills is even a real concern. I cannot overstate the importance of reading to children and the profound developmental impact—including comprehensive general knowledge and the strengthening of parent/child bonds—that comes from doing so.

A willingness to talk to children about anything and everything, regardless of whether they have a speech delay, helps their language develop and brains grow. As foster parents, we attempt to teach parents that even silly chatter with small children is a beginning language skill and an important step to cognition (or thought process) development. We use our time in the car together to discuss the trees, the trucks passing by, bridge construction, colors of birds, and the difference between a sunrise and a sunset. We have learned from therapists to emphasize the use of concepts, such as how the concrete truck helps in the building of the roads, why steel is needed in the construction of a bridge, or why it is important to know that the sun rises in the east and sets in the west. At the pre-supper hour, we talk about ingredients, bowls, measurements, and milking a cow, which, using our imaginations, usually leads to our rendition of "Old McDonald Had a Farm." Children's speech and language will grow through talking, listening, singing, rhyming, and imitation. All these types of singsong bantering will soon result in the rudimentary ability to babble or speak back. That is how language starts!

One of our more recent placements was a twelve-month-old little one named Wesley, who was removed from a profoundly neglectful environment. He used various tones of high-pitched screaming along with hand gestures to make his needs and wants known. At first, I was not sure if he was in pain, as the sounds were so unexpected. His older brother caretaker, who was also placed with us, was able to interpret the different meanings of the sounds. Over the next month, because we talked nonstop to him and demonstrated simple American Sign Language motions along with the words, Wesley completely stopped his screaming. I was amazed at his personality transformation and at his increased ability to communicate his needs now that he had learned more effective language skills.

Children with hearing impairments often have speech and language delays. One of our mute children, Braedan, age two, initially grunted and scowled as his way to communicate a greeting. For a while, we had to explain that gesture to others until we could finally teach him to use a smile and show a simple salute gesture for hello instead. Finally, a school that specialized in his specific deaf/mute issues was found and opened his world with a specialized curriculum that taught formal sign language and gave professional speech instruction.

Many children will qualify for speech and language evaluations, but be aware that even if your foster child qualifies for these services, there are endlessly long waiting lists for almost every type of therapy. Skye was sixteen months old when she was placed on an infant speech therapy waiting list. For twelve months, her mom and I took turns calling every month or two to check the progression of her spot on the list. The speech staff finally said yes there was room in the infant speech class, but now at two years and four months she had actually aged out! We pleaded with the staff that those remaining eight months were still enough time for her to begin class and learn something, but they disagreed. Hospital policy did not allow children over two years old to start the program. As is often true in foster care, others hold the power.

In the meantime, Skye's mother and I took it upon ourselves to improve her developmental level by spending time exposing her to as many new learning experiences as possible. We discussed the sights, sounds, smells, touches, and tastes she experienced. In this case, Skye's mom, her Help Me Grow worker, and I worked together to mesh and adapt our homemade therapy to what we thought the child's current developmental needs were. We mutually agreed to do similar activities in each of our homes, and some activities—like home-based Early Intervention class—we did together in my home. We did not have all the answers, but we brainstormed and did the best we could with the resources we had. While the formal infant therapy class at the hospital probably would have been better, we did make strides working together with the common goal of promoting Skye's needs.

As we know, parents are children's first teachers. The knowledge base that children have by the time they are age three is largely determined by the knowledge, dedication, and ability of the parent. Some parents miss out on a grand opportunity to educate their children through daily interactions—such as actively playing make believe with the child or having reading time—because they do not understand the importance of these types of activities. Parents who intervene by spending time reading will help jump-start their child's language and cognition and will help them acquire an early love of learning. Further, reading skills are essential and affect every aspect of life from grocery shopping to buying a car and holding down a job.

Sadly, some parents are illiterate and understandably do not want others to know that they cannot read. To these parents, we stress that everyone has areas of difficulty in their lives, and it is okay to ask for help. In a scenario such as this, audiobooks can be a great tool as both parent and child learn to read together.

There is so much a parent can do to help children learn language. For instance, children taking turns with their little sounds, and your response back, is a conversation in the simplest form. We playfully mimic our babies by saying, "I'm going to do what you do. See, we are rolling the blue ball." This is a simple conversation between parent and child that is fun, educational, and helps bonding.

201

One little boy, Sam, wants to hear *The Cat in the Hat* every time I see him, even though a whole slew of books is available to him. The appealing rhythm of the story makes this a developmentally appropriate request and teaches him about language.

Sometimes, language impediments begin with the parents, and this affects the way their children develop. We have a hard time explaining this phenomenon to these parents because obviously they do not hear it. One family "ikes ue im in da umma mons" (likes to swim in the summer months). They all talk the same. Some days, we are really starting at ground level to understand both the children and their parents and to get their delays diagnosed and treated.

Malcolm came from a home in which both his mother and grandmother had severe speech impediments. The mother refused speech evaluation and treatment for him because she could not recognize the delays in her own speech and thought her son's speech was adequate too. In these cases, we do the best we can at home working on teaching age-appropriate sounds, words, and expressions while waiting for agency officials to get court orders for professionals to be consulted, as is what was needed in this case. Oppositely, little Tyson was cheerful, energetic, and articulate, but man did he know how to swear! He had a full vocabulary, but few of the words were fit to be coming out of his four-year-old mouth. This is just another example of how children learn to model their parents whether their parents realize it or not.

I have watched several mothers teach their children to scowl and growl to purposefully appear mean. I asked a young mom once why she taught this to her three-month-old baby, and she said this behavior helps protect them when they are on the streets when they get older. While there may be some truth to that statement, I asked her to think about the person on the other end of that scowl and how the gesture might be interpreted. We talked a bit about fighting words and actions versus words of cooperation. We discussed that there are social situations where this behavior will hurt the child. Most importantly though, we had a great conversation listening to the other's point of view.

Another day while I was waiting at the visit center for my foster children, I observed a similar interaction between a mom and a toddler of about eighteen months. This mom was shaking him back and forth saying, "You gotta be mean, you hear me, you gotta be mean!" I immediately tapped on the glass and got the attention of the room monitor because no child can ever be shaken, even in jest. This action can cause terrible brain injuries. We know a youngster who is blind due to a shaking incident he suffered as a baby.

I have yet to meet a parent of a foster child, no matter what their circumstances, who did not have a cell phone. Their chosen "language" is texting, which when done repeatedly minimizes their comfort using other forms of communication. Most families of foster children will text and ask me to communicate to the social worker for them about one topic or another, instead of calling themselves. I will attempt to answer their questions, so as not to be rude, but I also tell them their responsibility is to call or email the question or concern directly to the caseworker. I remind them that if a conversation is documented in email, the added communication will demonstrate to the agency staff a commitment to their case plan. Still, because verbal communication is out of their comfort zone, only on rare occasions will they follow through with my suggestion.

In the hopes that they will be comfortable and better prepared in social situations, we role play communication skills with our children. Appropriate communication skills will lead to acceptable social skills. We stress the importance of polite greetings, answering people's questions clearly, and saying please/thank you. All parents have the job of teaching children social skills, such as looking someone in the eye, speaking in an audible tone where they can be heard, and having a pleasant nonconfrontational expression about them.

Lamont had a loud, strong voice that was clearly audible when he was playing or goofing around, but trying to get him to speak up and answer an adult in an audible tone was trying on our patience, since clearly it was not a matter of ability. He seemed hesitant to voice his opinion about anything. Practicing social situations where he looked us in the eye and spoke in a voice loud enough to be heard (without hearing aids) took many months as we built his self-esteem and confidence.

Teens and young adults who solely use text messaging and social media for communication unintentionally stunt the growth of their verbal language skills. Attentive parents should use technology safeguards and boundaries to set limits on phone usage and social media influences to create more time for interactive opportunities. Teen Kaye had many social anxieties that she covered by staying silent and letting the world happen around her as she sat passively by. To communicate, she chose to text or draw. Coaxing her out of her extreme social shyness took us training family and friends to politely wait for an answer when addressing her rather than covering up the awkward pause or jumping in to answer for her. Months of building her up emotionally were needed before she started to express even a few opinions. Encouraging children in the proper use of verbal communication skills will help empower them to become better prepared for the social demands of the adult work world. I am often heard saying to teens that a smile, polite attitude, and strong verbal skills are the important qualities that employers are looking for; job skills can be taught.

The other main category of developmental delay is physical, which includes both gross motor and fine motor skills. Gross motor delays refer to decreased strength in large muscle groups due to weak muscle tone, poor stamina, or chronic medical conditions. Weaknesses we have seen range from simply being clumsy to those who could barely move due to excessive time confined. We have also seen children with underdeveloped muscles, which results in decreased strength. Formal physical therapy is sometimes recommended, but I always ask a pediatrician for input on home strengthening ideas that we can also do with the child. We then create fun gross motor skill activities appropriate for the children. We like to build on the child's interests, such as using exercise balls, tumble mats, a balance beam, and all kinds of sports and outdoor play. These all make developing gross motor skills fun.

Our sixteen-month-old foster twins had different levels of gross motor development when they arrived. While Rosie was on target with toddling around the house exploring at will, Reagan was in sloth mode barely pulling himself up on the furniture. To promote his muscle strength, we decreased the time and frequency that he would be carried places. We took his two hands instead and walked him slowly anywhere he needed to go, and we'd sing a silly, "walking, walking, walking" tune. Over several months he got stronger and was soon running down the sidewalk ahead of his sister.

Fine motor delays affect smaller muscle groups. This type of physical delay can also result from inactivity and inexperience. We have parented many children who, even at age six, seven, or eight, have never tried to cut with scissors. Their hands are weak and uncoordinated. They require instruction in and demonstration of activities that are useful in correcting these small muscle weaknesses, such as working puzzles, stringing beads, building with blocks, or cutting with scissors. There are hundreds of other simple tasks that encourage hand/eye coordination, dexterity, and strength. On a positive note, at least the hours children are playing video games are helping with hand/eye coordination and aid in correcting some hand weaknesses.

Three-year-old Lonny had severe physical delays, both gross motor, which affected his coordination and ability to crawl, and fine motor, which decreased his ability to hold objects in his hands. His difficulties were due to a genetic condition that had global effects, meaning it caused developmental delays in many areas. One homemade physical therapy exercise that Lonny enjoyed was scooting on his tummy toward his favorite colorful textured balls that we would place a short distance in front of him to encourage better movement. He was such a little fighter who inspired us with his determined Army crawl as he tried with all his might to get himself closer to those toys. Through many daily practice sessions, he was encouraged and cheered along until he finally mastered the skill of reaching his destination. I will never forget the first day he successfully traversed the two feet of carpet to reach that beloved green ball of his and rolled over with it clutched to his stomach while squealing in delight.

All kinds of communication and physical delays are a direct result of abuse and neglect. For instance, a sibling group of seven children was found in a home secluded from neighbors where the parents were failing to meet their basic level of care for years. The children's neglect was severe and included them being kept "safe" in one of several locked rooms in the house. They were not often let outside to play or interact with others. This level of seclusion harms children in many ways and leads to decreased physical, emotional, and social maturity. These children experienced anxiety, depression, fear, and gaping developmental delays as diagnosed by school and healthcare professionals. Their hindrances were so extensive that they spanned many areas of their lives. They were malnourished and had physical delays with weak muscle tone in their legs and arms. They were uncoordinated when trying to run, awkwardly held their toothbrushes, and struggled with assembling the simplest arts and crafts. In addition, their speech, language, and cognition levels were profoundly low, and each scored behind their chronological age by two to three years.

Families of any child with developmental delays must stop ignoring the gaps their children have and instead concentrate on learning about the issues and correcting the deficits. Specifically, adults involved in the care of foster children must make the time for these developmental evaluations to be scheduled so that the details of each child's needs can be accurately identified. Though foster parents initiate the therapies, it is just as vital that the biological parents continue to attend the appointments when the children return home. Unfortunately, we have seen too many people get caught up in the emotional loss of not having the perfect child and wanting to pretend the problem does not exist. Parents must learn to support their children through their developmental journey. None of us is perfect. We all have struggles, and we all have our gifts.

CHAPTER 18: ADVOCATING FOR THE FOSTER CHILD

Foster parents place a high priority on advocating for foster children's needs. There are many hats to wear in this role, including being a caretaker, nurse, dietician, tutor, protector, and mentor. In addition, issues known at the time of placement as well as those found along the way need addressing. Obvious baseline needs such as food, shelter, medical care, and education are expected. However, going the extra step to wholeheartedly advocate for the child will differentiate between a good and exceptional foster-care experience. Some people see foster care as long-term babysitting, but most foster parents want to go above what is considered baseline care to provide excellent care for the children.

There is a difference between feeding a child food and teaching them about nutrition. I bring this up because so many foster children have not been well fed. There can also be a knowledge deficit about exactly what is healthy to eat and what is not. Most foster children are used to drinking soda and juice; few drink water. Artificially sweetened cereal and high-sugar condiments are the norm. We help children and their families understand that they absolutely need to strive for good nutrition to encourage proper brain growth, and this includes much less sugar whenever possible.

Families of foster children often bring high caloric, processed snacks and colorful juices to visitations because convenience stores readily stock these items. Even though these stores are convenient, unfortunately not all have healthy food options. Still, we advocate for the child in this regard by ignoring commenting when junk food is provided week after week and instead readily offer compliments to the family if a nutritious snack is brought. Libby's dad started bringing chili and fresh cut vegetables from granddad's house to have supper with her at visits. We made sure to make a big deal of this positive change from the usual sticky bun treat.

Families may lack a nutritious diet because they simply do not know the importance of eating less sugar and providing vegetables, lean proteins, and healthy fats instead. Others may lack funds for groceries or run out of grocery vouchers before the end of the month. Still others do not have cars and have to use public transportation to get to the convenience store. Young moms have explained how difficult the shopping chore is with little ones and strollers to maneuver on the bus. Some are forced to shop every day because they can only manage one bag of groceries at a time with their children in tow.

Nutrition does influence the brain's growth and development, especially in the first three years of a child's life. Nerves grow and connect, affecting how the brain thinks and feels. These connections are responsible for sensory interpretation (information learned through sight, sound, smell, taste, and touch), decision making, and the ability to control impulses. We want to provide healthy food options for our foster children because well-fed brains have the best chances at learning from the environment around them. Little Rose would come home from daycare simply wilting. She was cranky and droopy. I told the staff that I would send an additional afternoon cheese snack and water bottle for her because her little body appeared to need more sustenance in the midafternoon than was being provided. This adjustment seemed to be the key because she came home energetic and cheerful.

Advocating for children sometimes means taking their side as a show of support for them and their experiences. Many foster children can have a habit of hiding food because it may have been scarce at their home, and they learned this tactic as a means of survival. I tell the children that they are resourceful and smart, that I understand why they hide food, and that it is not something to be ashamed of. They become less fretful as they settle into our home routine knowing that food is readily available. The topic of needing to hide food usually subsides on its own.

Two of our little ones were genuinely afraid of a food shortage. Even though they ate a full meal, they would cry when the food was cleared away after suppertime. Apparently, the children used to scavenge through garbage to find food that they would then share with each other. After we learned their social history, we were better able to understand what was happening. We learned that the day they came into foster care they were found digging in a hole in their backyard searching for food. Unfortunately, drug paraphernalia was also found nearby. The children were only one and two years old at the time. Once we learned about this information, we allowed a small baggie of dry cereal to be on the shelf near their beds and always answered their requests for food with some version of yes. They stopped hiding food. I am relieved to say that they, as adopted teens, are strong and healthy and do not have residual food issues.

Physical exercise goes hand in hand with good nutrition. Parents of foster children are dealing with many other issues, so the need for exercise is often considered of low importance. However, as foster parents, we still hope to teach as many good health habits as possible in the time the children are in our care. This means teaching the importance of physical exercise and the role it plays in overall health. Many of us, as adults, must work toward being physically active every day because we did not understand the importance of physical activity when we were children. What a gift for a child to develop into adulthood with a good understanding about the right food and exercise balance needed for their bodies. Every single good habit a child learns builds part of the foundation of who they are.

On the flip side, every bad habit that we steer children away from also builds who they are. We discuss how someone who cares about their physical health might be less inclined to succumb to temptations that would negatively affect their body or mind. Having a healthy body and mind leads to better self-esteem, which promotes confidence in saying no to peer pressure and other chemical vices. I wish every child could have a caring adult in their formative years to boost them physically, emotionally, and psychologically instead of fighting the monsters of addictions that occur if they start using.

Our good health advocacy also includes many lessons on hygiene. Children who are well groomed the day they come into foster care are rare. When new foster children are placed in the home, we explain our family's hygiene routine to them and listen to what their usual routine consists of too. We help to adjust any bad habits and praise their good efforts. Some in child welfare will say not to worry about showering/bathing the first night the children are in foster care because they are adjusting. I disagree. Having children shower or bathe may save you from a dismal round of pesky bugs and various skin conditions. This in turn saves the child the embarrassment of bringing critters into the home. Trust me on this one.

Eight-year-old Maya taught me a great deal about lice. She had not been able to treat her own lice the day she came into foster care because she ran out of mayonnaise on her four little sisters' heads of lice the day before. She told me that this treatment worked "way better" than any other creams or shampoos that are bought at the store and did not cost as much. She is right; it does work very effectively! I have used mayonnaise and plastic hair cap covers for lice ever since!

We watch all children brush their teeth. This is needed initially because oral hygiene can range from lacking effort to plain nonexistent. We tell all children to think of their mouth as a house. We instruct them to clean the upstairs floor inside and out and then move to the downstairs floor inside and out. We demonstrate the importance of brushing their gums gently in vertical strokes, not vigorously back and forth. Getting children established with routine dental care is not only about a nice smile but contributes to their overall health. Many people do not understand that proper dental care, good nutrition, and even heart health are all related.

Omar, Tianna, and Jeremiah had very poor oral hygiene and suffered from bad breath. They informed me that they only had one toothbrush, which they shared at their grandma's house, and that they only visited there occasionally. They cried because they were not used to the feel of the toothbrush, and their mouths were tender and bled after brushing. Upon exam, the dentist found several rotting teeth on each child. All endured dental extractions, fillings, and sealants. We worked diligently after the initial problems were fixed to teach them proper oral care.

Upon arrival at our home, ten-year-old Destiny had black holes in three of her teeth that were large enough for her to put her finger into. She complained constantly of pain until those teeth were pulled. Even after explaining the urgent situation and sending photos to our assigned dental clinic, they gave me an appointment for her new patient exam three months down the road, as this was their "first available." Landing an earlier appointment involved me calling several dental offices that I knew, and one had enough pity on us to give us an appointment the following week. Thanks Dr. G and staff! Many months of direct supervision were needed while Destiny brushed her teeth to teach a skill she should have learned years ago. We explained to her that good dental health would mean overall better health for her during her lifetime.

Advocating also includes teaching good bathing habits. Proper hygiene has to be taught to some and encouraged in others. Most preteens and teens should shower daily. We hear lots of excuses that their routine is to bathe only once a week (or month), but frankly we explain that all armpits and bottoms need to be cleansed more frequently. Different skin and hair types do have different needs, but always some form of daily hygiene is needed. Skin and hair might need oil added, while others need the oil washed away. Children with drier hair types can sleep on a silk pillowcase or wear a silk cap to keep the cotton bedding from pulling moisture out of their skin and hair. Oils and lotions can help with drier skin and hair needs. I ask the child's family for guidance, and if needed, I ask the doctor for advice.

Our pediatrician has seen countless unhealthy skin conditions in our many foster children. She recommends gummy fish oil supplements for many children to improve their skin and hair health from the inside out. Little four-month-old Johnnie came to us with terrible eczema and scaling on his scalp. As scales would fall off, his head would bleed. He was constantly trying to scratch his head with his tiny hands because his hair was thick and dirty with dried blood and dead skin. I had to get permission from the agency to follow the doctor's orders to shave his head so antibiotic and steroid creams could be applied directly to his scalp. Within twenty-four hours, the condition had improved significantly, and he snuggled and cuddled every time we applied the medicine and gently massaged the areas. He started sleeping better, and his little four-month-old smiles and coos showed that he was clearly grateful for the comfort and relief.

One personal pet peeve of mine is needing permission to trim a child's hair. While I understand that a full haircut or drastically changing the style should need permission from the foster child's family, a trim is just good hygiene. Child welfare staff do not give families of foster children the right to refuse teeth brushing because they would prefer that we do not partake in that particular hygiene activity with their children. That would be considered neglectful. Having a hair trim for hygiene purposes should be the same way, especially when the hair is matted, infested with lice, or has some other problem, as has been the case with many of our foster children.

Some of the worst hair I've seen was on a set of five siblings who came to our home with dirty, unkempt, and unhealthy hair. A few of the children had large, tangled masses that encompassed much of their hair, and one had her hair completely entangled into a hair net. With permission, she had to have the entire hive-like mass cut off as the bundle was infested with lice. I ended up taking these children to my local salon who, God bless those stylists, called in extra staff so each child could have their own beautician for their special hair salon day. The severe hair problems were painstakingly dealt with in a respectful and fun way. The children had clean, combed-through hair and were all smiles when we left four hours later. One said to me: "It's so soft, Foster Mom! Look how pretty I am!"

The staff at hair salons are experts and will recommend what remedies to try. I buy small quantities of products because what works beautifully for one child may not be tolerated by another. Even children in the same family can have vastly different skin and hair-care needs. One family of eleven consisted of mostly half-related siblings and many parents, resulting in a wide variety of skin tones and hair types. Because variations like this occur, we keep a small stock of many different hair and skin products for the children to choose from.

Girls' hygiene needs require thoughtful conversation. I talk to our preteens and teens openly and explain that teens' bodies need special care. I also explain that it is okay to ask any questions. I let them know that I am a nurse, so I have heard it all, and they do not need to feel embarrassed to talk to me. After stating this, one teen promptly asked, "Okay, can you tell me the difference between an athlete and a virgin?" and so I did. She thanked me and said she had always wanted to know. I thanked her for opening up to me. This was the beginning of many diverse topics of conversation that both she and her sister had with me.

I like to get potentially embarrassing topics out in the open with a matter-of-fact chat that is done within the first day or two of children coming into foster care. I find out where their health and hygiene knowledge baselines are and provide additional information from there. I take my teen girls, who have started their cycle, to the store and let them pick out a few special soaps and products that they would like to use. I let the boys pick out a nice-smelling deodorant and cologne. The few extra dollars I spend are worth having them be excited about nice products they will use, which promotes better hygiene. We pack an emergency kit of sorts in the girls' school backpacks with a few clean-up items and fresh clothes to be used in case of an unexpected need.

Quite frankly, this is a good time to teach teens what a breast exam is and why it is important to do one each month. I tell boys that they actually can get breast cancer too. I inform boys that testicles should only have one ball on each side and to tell a responsible adult if this is ever not the case. The conversation does not have to be long and drawn out; just a few matter-of-fact sentences to educate them is enough. There is a chance that no parent will ever talk to them about these important health issues, and your brief education may save a life.

When I take a young child to a WIC assessment appointment, I advocate for having the child placed on the monthly recall schedule (instead of every second or third month) for serial height and weight measurements. I do not do this because the additional appointments are convenient for me to take the child to but because, when the child goes home, they will continue to have that monthly follow-through checkup. At these appointments, small children are undressed for their measurements, and the nurse naturally completes a skin check. The idea is for professionals to be involved at timely intervals to promote the best care possible for the children's general well-being both while in foster care and when they go home.

One phenomenon we have seen in the eyesight of at least a dozen children is their inability to judge the correct distance they are from an object. Either they take a huge step over a curb, or they frequently run into sides of countertops and walls. In every case where we have noticed this misjudgment, the child has ended up being diagnosed with an astigmatism (a condition of the eye affecting depth perception) and needed glasses prescribed. Nine-year-old Jamal said he could not see well when he came to our home. We took him to the eye doctor for an evaluation and found that he was 20/800 in both eyes, which his doctor said is considered legally blind. Jamal was overjoyed when he finally got his very first pair of eyeglasses. He spun around and talked about the leaves on the trees, the ridges on the potato chips, and everything in between. His Medicaid benefits provided only huge, thick lenses that overwhelmed his little face, but he did not care one bit. That sweet child prized those eyeglasses.

Every year, I get a recheck reminder card in the mail from the eye doctor for Jamal, even though they know he no longer lives here. For several years, I called the placing agency and talked to the current caseworker and told him about the reminder card. He said he always knew what the call was about. My hope is that somewhere along the line someone is thinking about Jamal's medical needs and making sure he is getting updated glasses every year. If nothing else, I think about and say a prayer that day for him, his siblings, and their terrible eyesight.

We aggressively advocate for proper medical attention for every child. Foster children can lack consistent medical care for reasons that range from financial concerns to parents who simply do not understand the importance of routine care. Upon coming into foster care, all children will go to an agency-approved doctor to be evaluated for their general growth, development, and social/mental health needs. We report any suspected abuse—including marks, bruises, or scars—to the doctor and the caseworker alike. Accurately recalling, reporting, and documenting statements the children make about abuse or neglect is the best way we can advocate for protection of our foster children.

One couch-hopping mom was simply trying to survive living here, there, and everywhere with her two toddlers and her severe addictions. Routine yearly healthcare checkups never crossed her mind. Another mom told me she did not know her child was sick at all. He was her first child, and the young mom was uneducated about the child's medical needs. She did not have the experience herself, nor did she have another knowledgeable adult around to help her understand that her child was not progressing the same as other children his age.

Lastly, the chances of a foster child needing extra services at school are high. Advocating with the schools is of paramount importance for the child. I have found teachers to be an excellent resource. However, they cannot offer unsolicited suggestions as readily as they can cite what they are seeing in the classroom when asked. Time and time again, I ask my foster children's teachers what they are seeing regarding level of function, behaviors, and peer interactions. They are a wealth of information and can point foster parents to the right procedure for getting formal academic assessments requested, and if needed, an academic plan established. The real value in an individualized education plan is that the plan of action will follow children from school to school and will be updated at least every three years—a high priority for children whose needs have likely been met sporadically, at best, before coming into foster care.

One evening, we had a conversation with a staff member at the community pool to update our list of current foster children in the system. Days later we discovered how this simple organizational act turned into one of advocating safety for our foster children. Apparently, soon after the information had been updated with the staff member, she received a telephone call from someone asking unusual questions about our foster children. The caller wanted to know if the employee knew the children, which foster home they were in, and the days and times we typically came to the pool. The employee called to tell us about the unsettling phone call because she knew the special circumstances of our home. As a result, we were able to piece together who the caller was, and the information was provided to the proper authorities, as there were several outstanding warrants for arrest of these individuals for violent crimes. Sometimes advocacy shows up in unexpected places.

Teaching proper nutrition, the benefits of exercise, good hygiene, and providing excellence in medical care and educational evaluations is a tedious and arduous process; however, learning this level of advocacy is what leads to excellent care of foster children. Those of us who have been entrusted with the care of foster children are challenged to be tenacious advocates for each of them. These children have a great deal of potential and can rise as high as the opportunities we provide them.

CHAPTER 19: COPING

Learning to successfully cope with the stress and unknowns in foster care is a must for both foster children and foster parents. There is no telling how long a foster child will be placed in your care because the time frame is rarely known. My answer to those who ask me how I plan for the length of stay of foster children is that I am ready for anything from two days to two years. The two-day placements occur because the agency has identified an extended family member or kinship situation where an abbreviated home study can be completed, and the children quickly move there. Two-year placements usually consist of a twelve-month case-plan period plus two six-month extensions. At that point, a plan for a permanent home for the child must be decided. Those placements can then take an additional six to twelve months to finalize. In short, learning effective coping skills is a necessity because planning on a time frame with a foster child placement is nearly impossible.

Adults demonstrating how to react to examples of stress give children a guide to refer to rather than depending on explosive outbursts to get attention and help. That is why we have to have adequate coping mechanisms ourselves before we can expect foster children to learn to appropriately cope with their own stresses. We try to be good role models and talk to our children to show them what we mean. One real-life example happened when I verbalized that I was sad that the babysitter canceled because I wanted to go to lunch with a friend I had not seen in a year. After getting off the phone, I explained that I needed to take a time-out for a few minutes to allow myself to be disappointed. Kelly, Kym, and Katie—the foster sisters we had at the time—offered to be "extra good" and watch themselves so I could go out and sit on the porch swing for a while. I told them I appreciated their thoughtful offer and spent a few quiet minutes outside alone decompressing. When I came back into the house, they had all drawn me pictures. I was touched by their thoughtfulness and expressed how much better their kind gestures made me feel.

When children witness low-drama coping and problem-solving, they will consider calm releases too. We like to introduce our foster children to manipulating stress balls or forming putty, playing with a fidget spinner, or using the punching bag. Other times, children prefer quiet distractions like writing in a journal, reading, coloring, listening to music, or swinging. These techniques are meant to redirect the child's attention away from the stressors until they have enough time to calm down and get on with their day rather than having a long temper tantrum or pouting session.

Allowing our foster children to see that they are not the only ones in the family who suffer from stress helps them understand that we all have to cope if we are feeling sad or mad. Calming our feelings until the situation passes is a teaching moment. An even-tempered household routine, without excessive emotional ups and downs in response to stress, is exactly what many foster children have missed being exposed to. Traumatized children can even stall at one developmental age where they stop advancing in maturity due to stress in their lives.

Teaching simple coping skills helps foster children begin to overcome delays and move closer to reaching age-appropriate developmental milestones. Twelve-year-old Mitchell had thumb-sucking and bedwetting problems due to extensive time periods in isolation as a youngster. His older brother said their mom could not keep Mitchell under control, so he was locked up in an inner windowless bathroom of their rental home where his yelling and crying could not be heard. His coping mechanism was to suck his thumb. He explained that since there were no windows, and the light bulb had been removed from the light socket, it was dark, and he was afraid. We gave Mitchell lots of wide-open space to play and relax, his own control over lights, stress balls to squeeze, and fidget spinners to manipulate when he was anxious, as well as easily washable bed pads for quick hygiene clean ups. These calm interventions helped him to focus less on the traumas in his young life. As the months went by, his nervousness faded, allowing his kindheartedness to show through. He sucked his thumb less, and he excelled in watching out for others' safety. He currently wants to go into law enforcement to help protect other abused and neglected children. Mitchell is a real gem of a boy and a great example of resiliency.

Lying is a familiar negative coping mechanism relied upon by many children. Unfortunately, this is well known to them as a way to deal with wrongdoing. Most children would rather blame a sibling or even the dog before facing the consequences of their action. When my beloved mother's lamp broke, I did not ask "Who did this?" as I likely would have been met with untruthful responses. I kept my stress in check and simply stated, "The lamp is broken." I then revealed the consequence: "There will be fifteen minutes early bedtime for everyone for the next three nights." The consequence, which will absolutely be upheld, eliminates the drama of sorting through who broke the lamp while allowing me to feel like there was a consequence for the disappointing action. If the guilty party comes forward, then I will adjust the consequence, but I will not fish for an answer. We also do not allow our children to get away with the blame game, and we ignore any silent-treatment episodes if they choose that coping mechanism.

While counseling is set up for almost all foster children, the usual frequency is once a week. Foster parents realistically need to find ways to help children cope using hobbies and distractions for everyday moments. Davy was a rough and tumble child, so physical exercise like shooting baskets and throwing a football were his thing. Miguel liked using the punching bag in the basement. Tre and Gabby turned to bike riding as their go-to activity for bad days. Our six little sisters enjoyed playing ballerinas in the playroom while listening to music. Cheyenne and Kym sang their hearts out to country music while tumbling on the play mats. All are great coping activities and seem to be effective mechanisms in regulating children's emotions.

Another stress reliever that works like a charm with every age group is water play. Babies love to splash in the kitchen sink while I am cooking dinner. Toddlers Skye and Nick were definitely big fans of this activity. Since discovering this go-to intervention, we have had no more afternoon colic in my house. Toddlers can always be talked into water fun with colorful measuring cups and containers. School-aged children love to take breaks using the slip and slide in the summer or taking daily sled riding runs in the winter (we finally found a positive use for our dreaded steep driveway). Preteens and teens can get over a huffy attitude in no time with trips to the community pool. Or, when all else fails, we ask them if they would like the first rotation for shower time that evening. This seems to calm their nerves. Water distraction activities rate high on our list of effective stress-relieving activities.

In addition, we have seen that exposing foster children to journals, painting, and working on crafts are all beneficial to decreasing stress. Abigail enjoyed sketching in the art book she received for her birthday, Avery liked to paint on canvases, and Audrey made yarn potholders. Every child will have different interests, so while one child may relax when reading a book, another may cry in frustration doing the same thing. Kisses and hugs are fine for little ones' boo-boos, but allowing school-aged children and older kids to discover ways to self soothe helps them prepare for time outside the protective walls of foster care where they will be making decisions on how to cope with the stresses of their lives. Our hope in teaching different activities of coping and in tailoring choices to each child is that they will be better prepared in the future to oversee their own stress resolution with harmless releases.

One day, while speaking with our teen foster daughters' dad, it became apparent that he lacked mature coping mechanisms and instead used a stream of cynical and bullying remarks with anyone who crossed him. He was immature in his curt and rude speech toward me every week at visitation. One day I found my bravery and spoke up. I reminded him politely but clearly that his two daughters were nearing their young adult years and asked if he would like young men to treat his daughters this same way. He hung his head and said, "Absolutely not. I'd kill them." We spoke further that his daughters were used to witnessing his negative behavior toward women, and they would likely choose to date young men like him as they aged, as that was what was familiar to them.[13] The girls were being raised to think that this disrespectful ownership behavior was just the way it was with all boys and men. He admitted that he did not like that thought. Over time, he worked hard in his men's therapy group and developed more grown-up coping mechanisms for his 38-year-old self. A year later, he showed nice improvement with his maturity. He had grown up fatherless and explained that this view was what he saw from the men in his life when he was young. As the years have passed, we have kept in touch, and he has matured into a very nice man who went on to raise his daughters to be confident young ladies "who command respect simply by the way they act." Witnessing this change with this father and his daughters is one of my favorite foster-care memories.

Teaching children to pray is an excellent coping mechanism as well because it gives hope. Many foster children have not had the opportunity to attend religious services, and literally others have never even heard of prayer. We are always pleasantly surprised that children of all ages and backgrounds want to talk about God. We start with the very basics. Most do not realize that simply thinking of God and talking to Him about a problem or concern is prayer itself. We teach the smaller children to pray a simple prayer: "God bless all our mommies. God bless all our daddies. God bless all our sisters and brothers. Make us good girls and good boys. Amen." We explain that "God bless" means we are wishing love, happiness, and safety on that person.

My papa taught us as children to say, "May divine promise remain with us and those who are absent" at the end of our supper prayer. We explain that this type of prayer reminds us to think lovingly about those whom we are not currently with, like their families. Foster children take great comfort in knowing we truly care about them and the well-being of their families, even enough to pray for them daily.

Eleven-year-old Tyreke said he had never been to church before. Being an extremely intellectual child, though, he enjoyed Mass and asked a lot of questions afterward. One day, he asked to borrow my phone and said he wanted to show me his favorite YouTube video and song that he listened to on his school Chromebook to relax. I allowed this, and he brought up a gospel rapper singing about God. The music was great. He told me he had never shared the type of music he liked with anyone before but, "because you go to church, Foster Mom, I knew it would be okay to tell you." I was delighted that we could share our love of music together on our drives to and from his football practices.

As another coping mechanism, we mention prayers of thanksgiving when reviewing the events of the day because doing so helps us to find something to be grateful for and takes the focus off ourselves and our worries. We will model by saying, "Thank you, God, for bringing these children here to stay with us and to be part of our family while their mom and dad get things at home fixed up." We hurdle help by starting the prayer if they want to try themselves. We say, "I am thankful for . . ." and let them finish the sentence. If they do not want to pray, that is okay too; however, we do not stop modeling finding an aspect of every day for which to be grateful.

We try to instill in our children the truth that God is with them always and that they can talk to God as a means of stress reduction and peace, day or night, locked in a "bad" room or free. The fact that God is always with them, in every situation and at every moment, is a remarkable thought filled with hope. We tell children they can feel comforted in every situation because Jesus is their friend, and He will never go away or leave them alone. One teen cried when I explained this level of love to her. As an only child, she said this thought made her feel less lonely.

Once, one of our teens was filling out a survey for a professional cognitive screening. She told the doctor that her favorite day was Saturday because it was "sleep-in Saturday" when she did not have to get up early for school. She further explained that Saturday also meant Sunday was almost here. When the assessor probed further, she said she loved to go to Mass with our family because she liked God and liked the thought of angels existing. She asked the doctor if he knew about God and angels and went on to say that she vaguely remembered going to church with her grandparents when she was younger. She told me this made her feel like she was closer to her family. Our frequently depressed teen said that more than any other activity all week long, she felt happiest when she was at church.

Overall, I believe children really like to go to church. I suspect the adults in our world are the ones needing to show a better effort in getting there, participating, and appreciating the true blessing of a bit of heaven touching Earth.

We believe that children can learn to deal with small failures and conflicts in a constructive way. Constant monumental reactions cannot be sustained. Just like adults, when children develop coping mechanisms to relieve stress, they will find that these methods help with the overall stabilization of their life. Taking on the formation of young ladies and gentlemen is the responsibility of all adults, but foster parents have an especially unique role to play in redirecting children's emotions.

CHAPTER 20: WORKING WITH FOSTER CHILDREN'S FAMILIES

Working directly with foster children's families can be very rewarding because doing so helps children stay well bonded to their family, even while they are spending time living in foster care. It is not possible to work with every family, such as those that have a violent past, an unstable drug-abuse history, or are incarcerated, but more often than not a relationship can be built and is not as intimidating as it sounds. We depend on an experienced social worker or supervisor to guide us with the decision on how to best engage the family. In most situations, foster children's families feel guilt, sadness, anger, and embarrassment toward losing custody of their children and understand that we are trying to help them.

Some families of foster children know the child welfare system well because they either grew up in an out-of-home setting themselves or have been involved with child welfare before as an adult. One set of parents met as teens in a foster home, got married at eighteen, and now their four children are in foster care. Others are new to foster-care rules, guidelines, and limitations altogether. They have not previously experienced their children being taken into the custody of the state. I can only imagine how awkward and sad that must be for them. Our goal is to meet each family with kindness and try to put their minds at ease that we will take excellent care of their children for the time they are in our care. The family of the child is typically nervous and afraid, so I extend the olive branch first. I help them understand that we know they love their children, and our family is not trying to take them away from them.

Foster parents who work directly with their foster children's families feel that, most of the time, the rewards of the experience outweigh the hesitations. One dad we worked with had several serious domestic violence charges. He was a large man who towered over me and who sported a glaring look anytime I saw him. At first, I felt worried and intimidated about working directly with him, but as we got to know each other better, he was actually very nice to work with. I never once felt threatened during our community visits. He was just trying to raise his children in an impossibly difficult environment. He eventually embraced working with a counselor whose therapy focused on the responsibilities of the father. Once good support, such as stable housing and employment, was put in place, he started getting his priorities in order and completed his case plan with the agency staff. He still texts me from time to time to send updates on how he and his four children are doing. He continues to hold down a job and has stable housing and a good extended-family support system. He bragged recently that he has gotten his children involved in sports activities on organized teams and that he and the children's great-grandmother are attending their games together.

After wasting years shying away from foster children's families, we now greet every parent we meet with cheerful openness and exchange cell numbers with almost all of them. I am open in telling them that we will take excellent care of their children while they work hard on their case plan and that we are rooting for them to succeed. I allow the children's parents to communicate with me by texting my phone (within reason) for occasional updates. I ask them if they would like to receive pictures of what their children are doing every day or two. I will pass along text messages from foster children's parents to young children and allow my older children to text or call from my phone from time to time. In all these years, I have only had one parent tell me no, he did not want to communicate with me or hear how his child was doing, which was unfortunate for his daughter.

One day, I left a message on our new foster daughter's hospital room white board. The message said, "Hello Skye's family! We are Kathleen and Ron Paydo, and we are going to be your daughter's foster parents. Our phone numbers are.... Please text us with any concerns. Take good care, and we will talk to you soon." Skye's mom later told me she knew that very first day after seeing my message that she would be successful in getting her child back because she knew all along that we were on her side. I try to remember that conversation whenever I am meeting new families. Small acts of kindness make a big difference in supporting the child, their family, and the success of the case plan.

I have found that offering communication first usually diffuses the anger that parents initially want to feel toward me as the foster mom. Right from the start, the families of the foster children are forced to look toward themselves as the reason their children are in foster care, instead of projecting resentment that the foster parents "took their kids". They can see that we are friendly, non-confrontational, and competent caregivers for their children. I portray an air of confidence toward my foster children's families and act as if I expect them to succeed, but I am ready if they do not. The parents feel helpless, scared, and alone in their battles, and while we cannot solve their problems, we can skip judging them.

As the weeks go by, we usually start to develop a friendly relationship with the child's family. We often go to medical visits together providing the best care for the child between the two sets of parents, as we both hear the same information. Appointments are less awkward if we are on good terms with each other. I am careful to keep the goals of the case plan as a guide toward all the work being done with the family. A foster parent's responsibility to the child is taking excellent care of them; boosting the family is secondary. I let the family know one of my responsibilities is to document how the child is doing, including any interactions at visits with the parent that I witness. I explain that I email caseworkers regularly with any information necessary to take proper care of their child. I implore them to do the same.

We know to be aware of the manipulation factor that can exist when, at times, the family of our foster child tries to play both Ron and me against the caseworker. We do not allow ourselves to be drawn into that drama. We find it best to compartmentalize which areas of each case are appropriate to be involved in and keep clear of the others. We use emails to accurately communicate what was said in a conversation with the families because, over time, the details are often forgotten. The foster parents' main role is to provide great care for the child and then provide accurate documentation of that care. The role of the caseworker is to head the entire effort, and with the direction of the agency supervisors and court personnel, make the decisions. We are the child's caretakers, advocates, and cheerleaders, but we stay in our lane, keeping the lines of who does what job clearly marked.

Family members of our foster children have, at times, tried to avoid their caseworker or hide information from them. We explain to the family that being in touch and readily available to the caseworker is a better strategy to help their case plan. Even though they are told this repeatedly by agency staff, families of the foster child often elude phone calls and refuse to stay in communication with their child's workers. This practice does not bode well for their case plan.

Eight-month-old Corbin suffered a fall out of a playpen during an approved afternoon visit at home with his family. The child was crying inconsolably at the designated pickup time. The parents pleaded with us not to "tell on" them. This request of course is non-negotiable. The parents of the child were encouraged to come with us to the hospital and follow through with getting the child proper medical care, which they did. The child did suffer a closed head fracture. Thankfully, it was deemed mild, and he needed no additional medical care except observation, but the incident was properly assessed and documented by the hospital staff. Modeling appropriate parenting skills by getting immediate medical care, informing CSB of the incident, and not covering up the event is the proper protocol. We doubted whether falling out of a playpen was even possible for a child who was not yet standing independently, but since the pediatric emergency room staff deemed the fracture an accident, the incident did not stop the progression of the case. Several months later, the child's parents did work their case plan well enough to meet the "minimum standard of care" for him, and he was returned home. Learning to deal with these types of doubts comes with the job; we rely on daily prayers for the children's safety after that.

Occasionally, when disagreements arise while working with the families of the foster children, we concentrate on discussing the problem but do not engage in arguments or confrontations of any kind. One dad did not trust me or the case manager on any level. No matter how nice we tried to be to him, he was always primed for a fight. He treated Ron and me in a sinister way, always questioning us with a distrusting attitude. It seemed as if he thought we wanted to adopt his daughter away from him, even though we assured him this was not the case. I walked away from his aggressiveness at visitation pickup and drop-off more than once and eventually had to request that the Sunday community meet location be moved back to the agency parking lot where video recording of all happenings occurred. Foster parents are gracious, but we do not have to go so far as to let ourselves be mistreated. We always have the choice to alter the environment or refuse community visitations altogether if needed.

An unexpected turn of events that evolved as we started working more with the family members of our foster children was the realization that we were often needing to parent the parents too. Many may not have had strong parenting role models to look up to in their formative years. They are likely raising their children in much of the same ways they were raised. When possible, we attempt to help these young parents interpret and understand child development, provide a few useful parenting skills, and demonstrate social niceties. For example, I spend a great deal of time sitting with foster children and their parents in the waiting rooms of doctors' offices. I encourage them to try reading a book to the child instead of constantly scolding their children for wanting to play on their cell phones.

Foster parents can also support families of foster children by encouraging them through their case-plan objectives, including teaching the importance of maintaining a routine schedule where visitations are not missed, how to make and keep all medical and counseling appointments, demonstrating effective communication skills, and modeling positive parenting techniques. My condensed "go-to tips" for parenting techniques are to attentively engage the child in play, and when necessary, distract them or redirect unwanted behaviors. I emphasize that follow-through matters every time. I also discourage the use of social media during childcare hours. These interventions are designed to help families of foster children feel less stress because they are demonstrating better control of themselves and their children through acceptable parenting skills and therefore meeting an objective of their case plan. Many appreciate the help.

Skye's young mother was committed to learning appropriate parenting and medical skills for her daughter. Throughout the case, I offered suggestions and reviewed her knowledge of parenting tips and strategies that I often used with little Skye. Skye's favorite activity was playing in her modified exersaucer—a tool that was needed to accommodate her delays and that allowed her the most freedom of movement. It even had special clip devices to hang her favorite toys. Skye's mom eagerly learned all she could about her daughter's medical care, including how to properly replace a feeding tube, should it become suddenly dislodged, and how to suction her lungs for respiratory distress. She demonstrated proper use of Skye's equipment, including how to troubleshoot mechanical failures on her medical devices. As mom and daughter had been granted increased visitation time together, we enjoyed several public outings together toward the end of the placement, such as walking around the mall together with medical equipment in tow. Skye remained well bonded with her mother throughout her time in foster care. The transition back home, along with her adapted exersaucer, was natural and non-stressful. I felt such satisfaction seeing this family grow, strengthen, and succeed.

Other times, families may find themselves struggling with rampant illegal drug use, which adds a significant level of difficulty to foster children's cases. Children are endangered when their parents' addictions affect their ability to provide a safe and nurturing environment. No matter what the circumstances are for a child to need foster care, illegal drug usage is almost always in the story somewhere. We have worked with families who are remorseful and truly want help to give up their vices for the stability of their family, while others will have no part of that.

A recovering addict once told me that she literally could not remember HOW simple tasks needed to be accomplished when she was under the influence of drugs. For example, she explained that she saw her baby crying and knew she had formula, but she could not think through the process of how to fill the bottle and feed it to the baby. In her words, "I wasn't aware if gasoline, vodka, or milk went in that bottle." After her children left foster care, she had another baby and fell back into drugs. I later heard that there was one day when she did not remember where she had left her infant. Her brother ended up driving by her on the street and told her the child was at Grannie's house, but the addict had no idea how her baby had gotten there. Apparently, she had left her there the previous day. Grannie later called to tell me about this incident, as she still considered me a support person even after her older grandchildren (who had been placed with us) had long since been adopted. This baby eventually ended up in foster care also. Sadly, drug addicts' vices are often too strong, and they can never properly care for their children again.

There are many different feelings that come to light for us when working with children from drug-addicted homes. On the one hand, we feel compassion and sadness for the circumstances the family has suffered, which has led them to drug use. We know they have suffered unspeakable trials and losses. On the other hand, those who work with drug addicts have heard every reason and excuse as to why they are in the predicament they are in and why they cannot stop using. One trainer, who has been working with drug-addicted adults for over forty years, says she would put the percentage of children taken into foster care as a direct result of parental involvement in drugs at 99.9 percent.

Foster siblings Lyndsey and Jacob came from a highly volatile home where the parents were chronic drug users. The children were aggressive and constantly instigating disputes with each other. I soon found that the children's mother had the same volatile temperament. She was not interested in cooperating with Children's Services staff, the case plan, or me. She was verbally aggressive and had a foul mouth, to her children and the staff, every time we were at the visit center. One day, as I entered the visitation center with Lyndsey and Jacob, their mom abruptly came up to within two inches of my face and started yelling at me that the flip flops she had gotten the children the previous week were not currently on their feet. I was startled, confused, and shocked at her aggression over their footwear. Almost immediately, I experienced a gentleman agency staff member, whom I have known for years, move just as quickly up into the mom's personal space and tell her pointedly, "Your children are in an excellent foster home. Now talk to the foster mom with respect." That one act of kindness years ago was a big deal and made me feel supported. I never forgot the incident or the worker's kind support. Lyndsey and Jacob were court ordered home sometime later, with a minimally successful case plan done. Now five years later, there are three more babies in the family, the father has committed suicide, and a concerned neighbor (an acquaintance of mine) tells me they are living the couch-hopping life again. Sigh.

I have worked with many young parents and extended family members over the years. They are not bad people, but they do make some bad decisions. Many also have developmental delays and sensory processing issues that affect their judgment. One drug-addicted mom just sobbed every time I saw her. I introduced myself and she sobbed. I touched upon the general ideas of foster care with her, and she sobbed. I tried to give small gentle suggestions about her child's significant medical needs, and she sobbed. I finally spoke to the child's grandmother, who appreciated my attempts and felt I went above the call of duty trying to help her daughter. Grandma shared that she was exasperated with her daughter too. That case plan did not work out favorably for the baby's mom, as she had too many personal needs herself and did not have anything extra left over for her child. After stabilizing at our house, her child went to an adoptive home. Thankfully, the adoptive family allows the stable grandmother to be active in the child's life.

Sometimes I have to directly advocate for the parents of our foster children. I know when I first started out in foster care, and even at times to this day, I think the agency lingo is over my head. I also know it is often not understood by family members of our foster children either. I have purposefully stopped in a meeting and asked for clarification especially in the presence of young parents. I would say, "I'm sorry, I don't understand what that means. Can you say that another way?" This discreet hurdle help past the problem gives an example of how to politely interrupt, demonstrates asking a question in a professional meeting, and gives clarity to what is being said. Families of foster children do not always understand the details of their case plan or grasp the seriousness of their situation. In an attempt to stick to time limits on meetings, agency staff talk very quickly and in their own language. Sometimes I think they do not realize how incredibly foreign their words and phrases sound to others. Being a liaison is a significant role that foster parents play.

One day, during a quickly moving family team meeting with a young mom and dad, I asked to pause the meeting for a moment, as I saw the mom and dad sitting in their chairs with blank stares on their faces. The lingo was obviously very much over the young parents' heads. I asked them if they understood what "adjudication" meant or what "PC" stood for. They said no. The moderator explained in much simpler terms that adjudication was the process of the agency proving the case in court and that they had a year to work this case plan, with two possible, but not guaranteed, six-month extensions. If they chose not to work the plan, then the agency would be forced to look for an alternative kinship placement and/or get permanent custody (PC) of their children. The mom asked if PC was the same as adoption and was told it was. Both parents started crying immediately. This young couple, who were barely adults themselves, were completely overwhelmed by all the terms and information being thrown at them. We had to pause the meeting for a time so they could regain their composure.

After the meeting, I told the parents that they had to learn to respectfully ask questions when they do not understand what is being said. They said they were nervous and afraid to talk. I received many texts from the mom and dad that night asking me the same questions about the details of the meeting. I answered what I could and also explained that I would email the caseworker to let her know what information she needed to clarify with them a third time. I strongly encouraged them to email her too.

There *are* parents of foster children who sincerely want to improve their lives and are willing to work through the objectives of the case plan to be a stronger family. The case plan may include taking domestic violence prevention classes or having drug/alcohol and mental health assessments, including successfully completing any warranted treatment. Individuals who get their records expunged, or cleared, and find employment can qualify for government-assisted housing, which helps stabilize their lives further. Some are serious about working their case plans so they can reunite with their children.

Being a cheerful motivator and reassuring the children's families that I believe they can succeed in meeting their case-plan goals will help give them confidence toward getting their children back. When given clear explanations and kind encouragement, parents will have a higher chance of staying focused on their goals. Not all families of foster children will embrace this sentiment, and I know that we can only do so much. When reunification time comes, I want to sit back with a clear conscience knowing we did the best we could to help each family. If the case plan fails, I take comfort knowing we were dedicated to helping them understand what was expected of them, that we encouraged their efforts, and that we took excellent care of their children each day they were in foster care. Ultimately, the final result is up to them.

CHAPTER 21: FOSTER CHILDREN DEPARTURE

When it is time for foster care to end, appropriate arrangements are made for the child to leave our foster home. Suitcases and duffle bags will be packed, and goodbyes are made as easy as possible for the child. Emotions will vary as much as children vary. Processing departures affects us—the foster family—in many ways as well.

Foster placements end for various reasons. The best-case scenario is that a child will be reunited with their family because the case-plan objectives have been met and the home situation has been deemed safer. Frequently, though, children are moved into a kinship placement where someone known to the child or the child's family has come forward, been approved, and taken the child into their home. Other reasons for a foster placement to end may be that the status of the case has changed to permanent custody, and the child will be adopted by either the current foster parents or another family altogether.

Whatever the circumstance, informing and preparing the child is incredibly important. The agency staff explains the process of foster care ending and handles the transfer. We, as foster parents, make protecting the child's feelings and bonding our goal. Emotional attachments are one element of foster caregiving I can have a big say in. Making sure the child knows how incredibly blessed we feel to have known them and that they will be forever remembered in our hearts and prayers is most important.

If reunification does happen, then the family of the foster child has met the case-plan goals to a minimum sufficient level of care and has gotten their lives stabilized enough to be reunited with their child. The child should be well bonded to their parents because they have likely been seeing them often. Ideally, visitation times increase incrementally in frequency and duration as the successful case plan draws to a close. The children are hopefully healed of physical injuries, have been counseled through emotional ones, and have increased in their age-appropriate school and independent living skills. The parents have been taught to understand positive parenting techniques and the use of kind discipline. These lessons are all designed to make the family happier and safer together again. Approximately fifty percent of the time this is the case, and foster children return to their families.

Even though many foster children will return home, transitions still put an emotional burden on the foster children. We work through the steps of what is happening with them. We support them emotionally, letting them know their family has worked hard to understand what brought them into foster care and knows better how to correct these issues going forward. As the foster family, we know that we have supported the agency's and court's goals that were set for the family to the best of our ability and made the child as strong as possible by getting their needs met.

It is also understandable that some children are apprehensive about going home. They have seen another side of both parenting and living now and may worry that the circumstances at home have not changed. We make sure that the child's counselors and medical staff are informed of any concerns and confirm that follow-up visits have been scheduled. We give a schedule of appointments to the family receiving the child and email the schedule to the case manager. We also offer to stay in contact with the family and children after they leave our home to be a support or an occasional babysitter for them. Many families take us up on this offer.

Fifteen-month-old Ella Sue thrived in the nine months she was in foster care. Her medical needs were met, and she was well bonded with both her mother and us. Her mother, Bunnie, cried tears of joy when the much-anticipated reunion day arrived. When we took Ella Sue home to her mother, Bunnie thanked and hugged me. She said her daughter coming into foster care was "both the hardest and best thing that ever happened" to her, because she was forced to leave a long-term abusive relationship and become independent and strong on her own. I watched Bunnie's self-esteem soar through the weeks and months of the case. Sadly, after promising to keep in touch, she never contacted us again, which is a realistic heartache of being a foster parent. We did end up with another foster child years later who lived in the apartment above Ella Sue and Bunnie. He told us, "They are doing real good," and said he rode the bus with Ella Sue sometimes. We miss her, but it is good to hear about her from time to time, and whenever I drive by their brownstone, I blow kisses her way.

Many of our cases have had children move from our home into a kinship placement with their extended family, coach, or neighbor. The details of the cases vary. Four of the children we do vacation respites for live in kinship care with a retired lady who had fostered their own young mom years ago. One family has three children, all of whom live with different support people: one with a grandpa, one with a coach, and one with a friend's family. The adults work to arrange visits so the siblings can stay connected in each other's lives, even though they do not get to live together anymore.

One inspirational kinship story is about seventeen-year-old Jenny, who had been recently placed in our friend's foster home. Unfortunately, this foster home was located outside her home school district. Later, Jenny's friend Valerie and her parents from the first school offered to get their home certified so the best friends could continue to go to school and play soccer together. This kinship home was a great match for the displaced teen, and she expressed appreciation for the work needed to get her moved there. Jenny was very happy when she was finally placed back at her original school with her familiar friends, coaches, and teachers.

Each 4th of July, we are invited to attend an annual holiday picnic with siblings whom we fostered years ago. While the children did not reunite with their parents, their kinship family invites us over for an afternoon full of fellowship, laughing, and reminiscing. Baby Clyde, who had yet to verbalize a single word in his first twenty-one months of life, finally said "bye" to me on the day he was leaving our home. His twin sister Marie replied, "Happy Birthday." It was not my birthday, but it is still a very sweet memory and one the family and I laugh about when one of us says "bye" and the other answers back "Happy Birthday." On this special visit day, the children hang all over us, which in this case I love. We know that the children were rescued from an unstable environment, healed, grew in our foster home, and are now again stable with their extended family. We exchange phone calls from time to time, not even about the children but just because our two families have become good friends.

If no reunification scenario is viable and adoption is imminent, then we at least have the peace of mind knowing we gave the case our best effort and taught the children many useful skills along the way. Thoughtfully planning to move the child to an adoptive placement means giving ample time for the child and families to adjust. Hopefully, the child has been bonding with the prospective family already, as it was becoming clearer that the case-plan objectives of the child's own family were not being met. When we find ourselves in this situation, we have a special family meeting that is appropriate to the age of the child involved. We use calendars to show timelines of visits, respites, and eventually the move date. If the kids are old enough, we listen to their opinion of when and how they want to move. Then we help them cross off the days as the move gets nearer so they can understand the sequence of events.

Typically, foster parents can help agency staff know when the child is feeling ready to move. In the case of baby Jessa, we were given the contact information about the chosen adoptive family by the caseworker and went to meet them one evening. Jessa then went for numerous visits lasting a few hours, to all day, and eventually a few overnights. After doing this for several weeks, the adoptive family and I thought the time was good for Jessa to move. I contacted the caseworker to inform her that both families felt the time was right. She agreed, and the transfer was arranged.

The transfer to an adoptive placement can be difficult and has happened with a handful of our foster children with whom we were particularly closely bonded. I tell the receiving family that when the big day arrives, I will say a brief hello and chat a moment or two but that once I kiss the child goodbye, expect me to leave abruptly. I ask them to do the same, with a quick nondramatic goodbye. This is the start of my grieving process as my own protective walls go up. I tell the family this ahead of time, so they know it is not personal toward them, but instead about how I have learned to cope with heartbreaking goodbyes over the years. Giving a child away—one who feels nearly like your own—is excruciatingly sad.

Not all departures are planned, and some children end up leaving as quickly and as unexpectantly as when they came. We have had two separate cases in our home where we received calls from the agency that an unexpected court hearing had been held, and "surprise" the children were going home that very day. In both cases, the children were back with their family within two hours of the notifying call. These are unusual circumstances, but it does happen. The only explanation given to us was that the ruling was "bigger than the agency." There is really no way to properly prepare the children for this situation. All there is time for is a quick announcement, a few simple affirmations about a job well done, some hurried packing, a rushed gathering of the Lifebook, and promises of continued love and prayers for them. Then you step back, take a deep breath, and pray that the seeds of knowledge you planted for the time you had them will take hold in one form or another. (We were told sometime later that one case had to do with an immediate jail release and the other with immigration.)

A planned departure of a few weeks or so is more typical when children leave our home. We draw pictures, write letters to each other, and finish their Lifebook of their time in foster care. Foster children are assisted in organizing and packing their personal items, toys, and especially gifts they have been given for birthdays and holidays. We prepare clothes, equipment, and medicines. We always pack children's treasures in totes and suitcases, not in trash bags. We share pertinent transfer information to all the child's teachers, medical providers, pharmacies, counselors, and therapists.

There are genuine feelings of grief when children leave our home. Certainly, some exits are more emotional than others, but all require time to process and adjust. In the cases where children have been with us a very long period of time, or any children we are particularly close to, it feels like having a broken heart, as I am sure that must be a real thing. There really is no other way to describe giving away a child because someone else says it is time. Grieving feelings for Ron and me include sadness, sometimes anger, and then acceptance. A therapeutic round of cleaning closets and cupboards usually ensues for me. The grief calms with ample time to cry, think, pray, and confide in our support people.

When a long-term child placement finishes, we usually take a break for at least a week or two to allow our own family the time to process the changes and grieve the loss of the child. We notify the agency staff on a date when we can be called again for a new placement (or sometimes they just call anyway). This open communication is helpful to the agency's placement department staff. One set of foster parents we know has fostered for twelve straight years with no breaks in between their placements. They say the timing just worked out that their cases kept overlapping. Those angels have some amazing stamina.

Teen Elijah called us several years after he left our home to say that he felt much better prepared to face adult life after his stay in foster care than in junior high school when he lived in turmoil with his mother. Even though his reunification situation was not ideal, he said the uncle he went to live with in kinship had been decent to him. He felt through our help, and his uncle's, that he learned some helpful life lessons that got him by in his young adult life. Not every reunification story is great, but we have to keep trying to plant the seeds of healing and growth in each child and hope it is enough.

Reunification day can be both a stress and a success. If we are personally unhappy with the reunification situation, then the transition leaves us feeling quite apprehensive. Honestly, a few cases that were coupled with bad transitions are haunting and last a lifetime. To survive the goodbyes, Ron and I have had to learn to compartmentalize our feelings and be a rock-strong support to each other. On the other hand, if we are secure with the stability of the home situation the child is returning to, we feel reassured and confident that we have done our part in bridging the family's reunification. Soon we will be able and ready to happily help the next child in need.

CHAPTER 22: SUPPORTING THE AGENCY

Foster parents will want to make sure the agency staff and court-mandated case plan are being supported to the fullest potential. The agency staff and the foster parents caring for the child are a team and support one another by accentuating strengths and compensating for weaknesses in each other. The goal is always to provide excellent care to the foster children. A lot of cooperation and work go into the critical relationship between foster parents and the agency staff. Though media reports do not often portray this, a lot of times it works very well.

Judging if the choices in the case plan are good or not does not fall under foster parents' responsibilities. This can be a point that upsets or disappoints some foster parents. Often, agency staff and the courts are making decisions based on additional information they have been given that, for confidentiality reasons, the foster parents will never know about. When I am feeling uneasy about a child's case plan, I make sure to document concerns as they arise, emailing the caseworker with the information, and then I intensify my focus on teaching the child as many safety tips as I am able.

I reiterate to families of our foster children what their caseworkers tell them, always stating the facts of the case plan and never my opinions. Essentially they choose to complete the case plan as it has been laid out by the agency staff or they do not; everything else is just talk. One mom did a lot of empty talking in the beginning of her case plan but then got serious and started earnestly working to get her drug assessment done and counseling sessions scheduled. She even completed an advanced-level parenting class on her own. In the end, her children went home. I had the opposite experience working with a young dad. He worked his case plan in the beginning, went to a few domestic abuse cession classes, and talked a big game plan but did not follow through. Ultimately, he chose his vices over his children and fled the state, leaving all his children behind.

Family members of our foster children ask us many questions, sometimes hoping to circumvent the caseworker. Again, referring the questions back to agency personnel helps them understand my role as a foster parent and the correct chain of command to the agency staff. Plus, it prevents information from being lost or misinterpreted. The family of the child has the ultimate responsibility to gather information from many sources (agency staff, court-appointed guardians, therapists, doctors, etc.), understand the needs of the child, and achieve the goals of their family case plan.

We ask our caseworkers for their cell phone numbers, and many will give them to us. Obviously, we are respectful to text only during business hours. If I want to speak to my foster child's caseworker by 4pm, I will send an email and a text at 8am asking if they would contact me sometime that day. If they have time to plan, they can usually call. If not, they will provide another time that would work. If a high-need situation exists, and I have not heard from the caseworker, then I call a supervisor. I have yet to be involved with an agency that has an adequate ratio of caseworkers to foster children due to the large number of children in care. For this reason, I am reasonable in my time requests of the caseworkers. I asked a worker once how many cases she was supposed to have, and she told me twelve. I asked her how many she actually had, and she told me twenty cases, for a total of thirty children. I know the chances of dialing a telephone number and getting to speak to the exact worker at the moment I need them are low, so I plan ahead. I am polite, respectful, and supportive to my children's caseworkers, as they are to me in return. Ron and I have worked with staff from ten different counties in our career, so we feel this is a good sampling of a successful way to work in the system. Cooperative relationships with agency staff make fostering much more enjoyable.

The licensed social worker or caseworker (not necessarily a licensed social worker) assigned to our foster child's case will also make a difference in the foster-care experience. In my opinion, some social workers would prefer foster families be less involved in the case and instead mainly take care of the child. Other caseworkers completely embrace foster parents working closely with them and deeply appreciate the foster parents' time and extra efforts. I talk to the caseworker assigned to my foster child's case and get to know their opinion and style. Typically, seasoned workers see the value in the extra ears and eyes that foster parents provide to the case.

Foster parents support the placing agency by communicating the details of the child's care to the caseworker. The effort of concise and timely documentation is greatly appreciated by most staff. Since caseworkers are not typically present at the appointments, there is value in having names, locations, and dates written down. Keeping up with every appointment of every child on their caseload is not possible. Proper documentation and results of appointments are needed for the child's case-plan record anyway, and my email notations can assist with these updates. I try to keep in mind that while I may feel busy keeping records on six children, they are clearly very busy if they are doing it for thirty.

Some caseworkers are straight out of school and have little hands-on experience in child growth, development, and behaviors. Many are not parents. As foster parents, we take the opportunity to support the caseworkers as they learn their new job. I have found new workers to be open when I offer kind support. The concern for their success can reveal itself in the form of better confidence of the young workers and possibly less job turnover. This leads to a more experienced staff who can provide excellent care to foster children with increasingly difficult behaviors.

The evening Ella Sue was brought to our home, she was delivered by a new social worker. She, the caseworker, was in tears because taking the child from her crying mother upset her immensely. We gave the young caseworker emotional support and encouragement during that placement event. As the weeks passed, I heard that the worker had left the intake unit for another job within the agency because she did not like having to take children away from their parents. Nine months later, when the case closed, and Ella Sue was safely returned to her stable home and overjoyed mother, I tracked down that young worker's phone number and told her the end result. I also shared with her that Ella Sue's mom said, "Tell the worker who came that night that having my baby taken away was the best thing that ever happened to me." The worker thanked me again and again for calling her with the positive news.

Foster parents work very hard, spend some insanely difficult hours with the children, and could benefit from higher reimbursements, there is no doubt. Of greater importance, though, are consistent expectations, accessibility, and supportive treatment from our caseworkers and their supervisors. The combination of experienced agency personnel and committed foster parents dedicated to sticking out the tough days together will be cost effective to our county budgets because they lead to less foster-parent turnover and fewer placement moves for our foster children. Social service directors face a job that is a huge challenge because foster children's numbers are increasing, and a way must be found to service the masses with the available resources. Thank God for the dedicated child public service employees and selfless foster parents who dedicate their lives to do an excellent job.

CHAPTER 23: FOSTER-PARENT TRAINING

Rules, regulations, and standards are important for foster-parent training, but sometimes they are not enough to deal with the realistic concerns of modern-day foster care. Theories and generalizations get foster parents thinking, but the real value comes in experiencing useful examples and demonstrations. Training support in the form of behavior-specific programs is needed to develop a higher skill set for the increasing challenges we see in our foster homes today.

Certifying and training foster parents is expensive, especially with the dishearteningly high rate of fifty percent of foster parents quitting after just one year of service or after one foster-child placement. While rules and regulations trainings are necessary, clearly repetitive training on vague concepts is a primary reason why many new foster families are unprepared when their foster-care experience goes live. Training that is more realistic and practical would be a better safeguard against foster-parent burnout. Frankly, the missing piece of training is answering this question: "What is it really going to be like to have strangers living in my home every day?" This question not being properly addressed is the reason so many foster parents quit.

In my opinion, the short answer to that question is that foster parenting is flat-out tough. Honestly, being a foster parent is partially a loss of your own life. New foster parents can be unaware of this reality and are shocked when faced with it. Most veteran foster parents will say to stick out the vocation choice because eventually a new normal will develop. However, many foster parents are so thrown by this overwhelming feeling of lost control in their own home that they cannot or will not wait out the transition time until that new level of normal is found. That's it. That is the big reason we lose that fifty percent. Now to find ways to fix this.

As a point of comparison, consider that social service agencies' top administrators are not inexperienced licensed social workers fresh out of college. They have years of skill, education, and experience to make them effective leaders. The same should go for foster-parent training. Hiring experienced childcare trainers to realistically prepare foster parents for the high level of service they are being asked to provide would be a more effective use of budgetary dollars. Foster parents understand that not all trainers can have many years of fostering experience, but they should have a great deal of realistic experience working with the various emotional, physical, and behavioral needs of children. While foster parents are being asked to up their game to take in higher numbers of children with more advanced problems, the quality of support and basic training remains the same.

Recently I heard of a new set of foster parents who are quitting after fostering a normal-needs baby for two months. Apparently, they decided that foster care was not what they expected and feel that fostering is no longer for them. If foster families are not taught enough useful skills and realistic expectations to make them feel comfortable in their own home, they quit the program. The cost and effort to recruit and train new parents then multiplies. When foster parents are so distraught after one child that they do not feel they even want to try again, we are forced to look for a better solution. The preparation process must improve, especially keeping the learned information fresh in the time frame between pre-service training completion and the actual arrival of the first foster child.

Getting advanced trainers who are experts in hands-on childcare from differing avenues of life would be the most helpful to broaden foster families' baseline knowledge. We are being forced to deal with more challenging behaviors in a more challenging time in our society. The most useful information presented to foster parents has to be tried-and-true actions that are effective for these difficult behaviors. Police officers, drug enforcement personnel, nurses, and group-home/residential facilities staff members have historically taught me the most usable information I have in my repertoire of parenting skills.

One memorable training that used to be offered years ago was given by a police tactics expert who worked with incarcerated teens. He taught foster parents amazing techniques in behavior management and in redirection. We learned that if an angry teen is charging at you, throw anything—a clipboard, a pen, or a set of keys—away from where you are standing, in the hopes of providing enough distraction and time to escape the room. The teen cannot help but be caught slightly off guard and look momentarily at the thrown item. Another idea is if we feel a child is a flight risk, we can lock away their shoes at night. A shoeless child will not get far and will be easier for the police to spot.

Furthermore, we learned that if a stranger approaches while riding a bike, we should keep the bike positioned between ourselves and the stranger so we can forcefully shove the bike at them should they try to attack. If approached in a parking lot, keep yelling loudly while running and throwing the car keys in the opposite direction. This approach forces the assailant to choose between an attack or getting the car. At the same time, the yelling is drawing attention to the area. If we find ourselves in a choke hold, we know to turn our head inward while bracing the attacker's arms up and away from our throat and quickly dropping our full weight to our knees. Ron and I took this training one time, twenty-five years ago, and thanks to the knowledgeable and interesting trainer, we still remember his creative and helpful techniques today.

Veteran foster parents can also be a source of practical solutions, and many are willing to teach future foster parents skills that go beyond basic training. I have heard repeatedly through the years that the most useful advice comes from other foster parents. When a crisis is occurring in a foster home, the foster parents may need to ask for immediate assistance from the placing agency. Unfortunately, agencies are limited in the help they are able to provide.

Planned respite time for known needs can be arranged ahead of time, but a crisis happening with no notice leads foster parents to figure out how to get through the disruptive situation on their own. This could be an area for agency staff to consider setting up a program, with appropriate compensation for veteran foster parents, to help. This help could come in the form of a face-to-face visit in the home of the distressed family where mentoring would be offered to de-escalate the disrupting child and support the foster parents. Offering to take the struggling child short-term into their own home as an emergency intervention might also be an option. Either way, new ideas need to be brainstormed.

Our foster teen Bailey slit her wrists superficially with a shaving razor one evening. I found her crying on the bathroom floor, sobbing about her persistent problems. I took her to the hospital where the ER staff asked her many questions regarding her intent. Whatever details Bailey gave the staff, they were satisfied that she was seeking attention and sent her home with us several hours later. We were young parents and felt inadequate to be responsible for Bailey's incident that evening or any possible future actions. Our calls to the agency hotline were not met with the degree of concern we felt we needed for her and for us that evening. So, all that was left to do was carry on for another day and talk ourselves out of panicking and quitting the program. We perceived this support as lacking, and that is all that matters when the situation is happening in your home. We felt alone on an island of uncertainty and worry.

Lists of contact information of individuals who foster for any given agency or even foster parents who reside in our own town are not given out for confidentiality reasons. Foster parents are tasked with networking to find each other as not everyone wants to pursue meeting foster parent supporters and friends online. We encourage veteran foster parents to initiate introductions to new families, especially when meeting face-to-face at foster-parent training sessions, because new families often state they feel shy and insecure about making the first contact on their own.

We approached a new couple at a training recently and asked them about themselves and their foster-care journey. They expressed relief that we came up to them because they were feeling overwhelmed. Later that week, the foster mom reached out for guidance about unusual behaviors they were seeing in their first foster son, and she expressed how much she appreciated having my contact information already handy. She said Ron and I portrayed a helpful and positive disposition when we met and made her husband and her feel more comfortable reaching out for help. They did not want to talk to the agency staff about their uncertainties regarding foster care because they "wanted to be seen as competent." All they seemed to need was a cheerful boost of moral support and a quick lesson in redirection to get them through the first few months of foster-care life.

One day, I learned a trick from another foster mom on how to keep pajamas on a two-year-old child who was full of mischievous behaviors at bedtime. He repeatedly took his pajamas and diaper off. She suggested putting the onesie sleeper on and zipping it up backward. "Then he can't reach the zipper!" I could not believe that would work, but she demonstrated, and the trick was flawless! All you have to do is twist the footie part of the pajama a little bit and zip the pajamas up the back. Problem solved. I have passed this ingenious suggestion on to many parents of young children who like to bare it all. Small supportive hints like this make each other's days easier.

Years ago, we did a weekend respite for a teenage foster boy named Joe. The veteran foster mom bringing Joe to me for respite told me to have him sit on the floor in the hallway with the bottoms of his shoes against the lower part of the bathroom door whenever I went to the bathroom. This way I would know exactly where he was for those couple of minutes. She told me to have my little girls sleep in my bedroom for the duration of the planned respite nights Joe was in my house to ensure their safety. Thank goodness for that veteran foster mother, her knowledge, and her excellent parenting skills in sharing these tips with me. As an experienced foster mother, she had the foresight to share these useful tactics to fill the gap of missing information from the agency respite request call. I was able to effectively care for Joe and protect my little girls at the same time. Creativity goes a long way in this line of work, which is why foster parents must share ingenious ideas with each other.

If you are a foster-parent trainer, please look at your curriculum and give foster parents a high level of realistic and practical parenting techniques and demonstrations. Consider training techniques besides role playing between one novice foster parent to another. Too many times foster parents must rely on other foster parents' experiences and knowledge when situations arise that we do not know how to handle. We are forced to depend on each other, too much so. Use examples from real-life situations that have useful techniques and rationale as to why they work. If the training does not improve, foster-parent burnout will continue.

All foster parents continue to face new challenges throughout their foster parenting career. Veterans in the business and strong trainers should step up and be a bridge to newer families' learning. After all, every foster parent was once "new" when learning the ins and outs of the fostering program. A supportive layering of love helps all people, including foster parents. One of the things that inspired me to write this book was the hope of sharing strategies that I (and others) have discovered through trial and error. Graciously sharing ideas with each other is what makes fostering effective and the experience gratifying.

CHAPTER 24: RETAINING FOSTER PARENTS

The need for active foster homes never ends. Retaining foster parents has a critical direct trickle-down effect on other departments. Having experienced foster homes can positively influence caseworker job satisfaction because there might be a decreased need to move foster children from home to home since veteran foster parents can typically manage difficult child behaviors. Another benefit in having veteran foster families is that they are often comfortable parenting large sibling groups. These facts, in turn, help the agency place fewer foster children in the more expensive fostering option of a treatment or therapeutic level foster home (or an even more expensive residential facility). Significant financial savings would occur by keeping already-trained foster families from quitting the vocation.

The reality is obvious. Our country needs more foster homes. Foster children and their families face increasingly serious issues. Drug use, mental health illnesses, and poverty are rampant. These problems, especially the opioid crisis and the sources of it coming into our country, are responsible for a lot of the blame for the huge influx of children into the system. Communications to foster parents urge, "Please consider children outside of your comfort zone. If you have an open bed, consider taking another child." Many foster parents will stretch to accommodate more children and then end up quitting because the pressures are too hard and the support too little.

Because the foster-care program is so near and dear to our hearts, we find it difficult to discuss its shortcomings, but we hope that, by doing so and by offering our suggestions, we might be able to effect change. Many foster parents are nearing retirement age and have given a good number of nonrefundable years of their lives to this cause. The need to replace these experienced foster parents in the system with fresh homes is a genuine worry for those of us who sincerely care about the future of the program.

If asked, I would say that feeling isolated, experiencing guilt when a foster-child placement fails, or fear of allegations are three key elements in why it is difficult to attract and retain foster parents.

Feeling alone in the day-to-day struggles of parenting foster children long term affects fostering satisfaction. Curbing our feelings of isolation involves coming to a full understanding that the placing agency is unable to help much with daily ongoing support. Chronically heavy caseload numbers carried by the staff prevent any one individual foster home or any one foster child from getting sustained support. Case managers, supervisors, and foster parents have to carry on the best they can with the resources they have. Most caseworkers would like to spend more time with the foster parents and foster children on their caseloads, but staffing levels do not allow this luxury. Therefore, the squeaky wheel gets the grease.

The feeling of isolation can be especially strong when inexperienced families impulsively decide to accept a foster child based on the emotion of the call rather than on their own natural gifts and talents. While agency placement workers encourage families to concentrate on which type of foster child would be a fair and reasonable placement for them, it just does not always work that way. An open bed is an open bed. We know that foster children and their problems are unique, but so too are foster parents and their strengths, and agencies must take these things into consideration. We understand that after the child is accepted and delivered to our home, the rest of the work is done mainly on our own.

Another reason foster-parent retention is challenged surrounds the situation when a foster-child placement fails. In other words, the foster child needs to be moved into another foster home or facility. This is called a disruption. Movement of children should be avoided as much as possible because it is difficult on the child, it can result in weakened bonding and trust issues, and it requires additional man hours from the agency staff. On some occasions, a move is not appropriate, but other times it is.

Disruptions can occur for several reasons. On occasion, children are placed in a foster home where the ability of the foster parents does not match the needs of the child. At best, appropriate foster placements will be challenging. At worst, inappropriate placements will lead to the need to move the child. Disrupted placements not only cause an unfortunate move for the foster child, but they also evoke intense feelings of failure for the foster parents and decrease the chances of the foster family staying in the system long term. If the foster child is not a good fit, then this initial experience can be especially stressful and may be the first and last foster child a family will ever take.

There are also financial implications to be considered when needing to move a child into another placement. Obviously, the needy child must be placed somewhere, so this is where the intake process is critical. Even if fewer numbers of children can be placed in level 1 county homes (the least expensive) the minute they come into foster care, placing the foster child who has an especially difficult set of behaviors in a therapeutic or treatment foster home from the very beginning may prove to be a better decision overall, as it decreases the chances of the child needing to move later. In other words, a child too difficult for a foster home should not be placed there to begin with. In the end, a more accurate placement process could help save heartache for the child and money for the county.

In reality, what used to be considered a child with "high needs" long ago is now a routine level 1 child—except that they are not. Perfectly matched placements do not exist because perfect people do not exist. No one is looking for a perfect scenario, but children whose needs nearly align with the ability and strengths of the foster home will lead to fewer disruptive placements, better retention of foster parents and staff, cost savings for the county, and a more successful experience for the child.

Teen Candace is a great example of this type of placement. Her full story went like this: She was accepted into our home because of the urging of the placement worker on a Friday at 4pm. No unusual info was given, just basic issues of school delinquency, lack of structure in the home, and neglect. When Candace walked into our house, she stared off into space as if she was in a catatonic state, crept around the house sneakily, was of exceptional size, and rarely spoke. At about the six-week mark, the situation had not gotten better. One evening, while I was driving the car, Candace opened her car door and tried to jump out of the passenger seat. We were on a two-lane highway going about 45 miles per hour. I pulled her back as hard and fast as I could and stopped the car safely, by God's grace. I was deeply shaken by the incident and was worried about the teen as well as myself, as I was largely pregnant. I took her immediately to the ER, and she was admitted to a psychiatric ward in a true catatonic state. The nurse on the floor knew Candace from a recent admission and told me that the agency staff was told at the last discharge that Candace's behavior made her too dangerous to be placed into a foster-home setting. Her behaviors made for a dangerous situation and an inappropriate placement for our foster home. We were too new to know. The agency had the responsibility to protect me and my family, but it appeared that needing a willing home with an open bed on a late-Friday afternoon came first. Candace was discharged a few weeks later to a residential facility. Surprisingly, we did not quit fostering that day and took another teen girl a week later. She was sassy and sweet but most importantly was an appropriate level placement for our home.

Getting more children placed in the best home the first time would not only decrease disruptive moves but would also increase the chances of keeping sibling groups (or extended family members, like cousins) together. We have had four sets of siblings come into our home who later were found to have siblings or cousins somewhere else in the system. We stumbled upon these sibling connections ourselves. I am sure there are many more that we never knew about. We took in one little boy, Tyrece, who was talkative and cheerful. During his bantering sessions, we noticed the mannerisms he displayed and the way he spoke were so similar to another little girl that we did respite placements for that we joked amongst ourselves that he sounded just like Coryalina. He heard and said, "You know Coryalina?" We said, "Yes, do you?" He informed us that she was his cousin. We had the social worker check the relationship out, and it was true. Tyrece was able to move to the other foster home that Coryalina had been placed in several weeks previously so that he could be with his first cousin. Moving him from the forty-eight-hour placement in our home to be with his same-aged cousin (whom he was eventually adopted with into the same home) was certainly better for his long-term bonding.

One "disruptive placement" was actually a well-thought-out and planned move for the children involved. Disappointingly, it was still documented by the agency staff to be a disruption, which is terminology that does not sit well with foster parents.

Young siblings Javon and Whitney were placed one evening in our foster-only home. A few weeks later, a new foster-to-adopt family, who had just gotten their license approval, started doing occasional respites for these young children. Over many months, as the new foster parents' relationship with the children grew, the respite family asked the agency if they could be considered for placement of the children, as the parents of these foster children had not visited once in over six months. The agency staff agreed that the direction of this case was indeed leaning toward a failing case plan and potential adoption, and they would approve the move of the children. The new family still worked the original plan objectives of family reunification but was also interested in the alternative plan of adoption should the case go into permanency. This decision allowed Javon and Whitney to continue bonding with the foster-to-adopt family until the time permanent custody was granted a year later.

The way the court system works, two, three, or even four years can go by until a case is cycled through to completion. After the case plan and extension timelines are deemed exhausted by the courts, foster children are found a permanent adoptive home. Javon and Whitney were lovingly bonded to these parents who did indeed end up adopting them. They had been thoughtfully moved into the foster-to-adopt home instead of sitting in our foster-only home for the additional three years that passed from the time they left us until their adoption day. Even though a move did have to be endured by the small children, their bonding greatly benefited in the end. Certainly, a one-stop fostering placement is the ideal situation, but oftentimes that does not happen, especially when children are suddenly removed from the parent's custody in the middle of the night and when open available beds are limited. These situations need strong agency leaders who are highly experienced and who take the time to consider the possible options. Kudos to the agencies that embrace this positive thinking instead of labeling it a disruption.

Another time, on a Friday afternoon, we took two children in when we already had three other foster children in our care. The placement caller asked for short-term help over the weekend until a long-term home could be found for the siblings with special needs. When Monday came around, the agency staff was having difficulty finding another foster home for the children with special needs, so we continued another week. By the second week, we had had some close calls regarding safety with the older boy who was profoundly developmentally delayed. At seven, he was nonverbal and kicked the other kids whenever they got too close to him. The last straw was when I was forced to jump up and grab a six-month-old away from the swing of his foot just before he could deliver a full-force kick to the baby's head. I do not think he was aware of what he was doing, but the potential lack of safety to the other foster children was too high. I called the agency staff and insisted they keep their word to get the brothers placed with a therapeutic level foster home. At that point, the agency staff agreed that the safety and stress issues were too great for us to provide care for all the children. Calling this situation a disruption was really a matter of semantics because the children were originally accepted under a weekend agreement.

Other times, especially in the case of older foster children, the children will purposely attempt to disrupt their own placements by provoking their foster parents in the hopes of being removed from the foster home. They mistakenly think they can control the system by exhausting all potential foster-home placements and get themselves returned to their own home sooner. We try not to be drawn into that drama. One set of siblings that was placed with us had four children who settled in nicely here. The fifth sibling had high hopes of manipulating the system and getting herself out of foster care and back home immediately. "The other kids can come home later," she told her caseworker and me. Numerous conversations followed about how difficult it is to keep large sibling groups together and to choose her decisions carefully because staying together with her brothers was a high priority for the agency staff and us as well. An attentive and experienced caseworker was able to provide our home the added time needed to work through some rocky days with the child and managed to stabilize her in our home with her sibling group intact until the day their family reunified a year later.

Realistically, when all coping mechanisms fail and the feelings of a disruption are occurring, we reach out to the case manager and their supervisor. We have learned to not wait until we are at our wits' end. We make the struggles known. Agency staff may suggest trying a short respite break or may schedule a disruption intervention meeting. Quite frankly, not a lot will change, and there is normally little additional help to be given. We ask anyway. It is hard not to quit. We have grit. We try again. We consult other experienced foster families for additional advice that may help in our situation. If the child absolutely must be removed, most agencies require a two-to-four-week notice. That is the reality of foster-care life.

One day, a disruption occurred because a set of older foster parents got a call about a twenty-three-month-old boy. He was placed in this couple's foster home because the placement call information had portrayed a walking and talking two-year-old, when in reality the child was severely delayed and was not ambulatory or verbal. He was floppy muscled and always needed to be carried. These older foster parents were unable to care for him properly in their two-story home due to their own physical limitations. As a result, this little fellow had to be relocated to our foster home because he was not a good fit for the first foster family. This was an unnecessary move for the child because of inaccurate information at the time of the initial placement call.

Sadly, the guilt placed on foster parents for foster children's disruptions is tremendous. Many foster homes are lost after the removal of a child because the foster parents felt as if they failed. Foster parents do sincerely try to manage surprise behaviors that come to light after the child is already placed in the home, but they cannot always manage them. Not all agency staff are supportive and gracious when this happens. Jamal and Lia, our two elementary-school-aged children, both of whom had very difficult behaviors, needed to be moved after four months of us trying to help them. When they were placed in an experienced therapeutic home after us, they disrupted again within twenty-four hours and were moved a third time in one week. The inability to properly care for a child is heartbreaking, but agencies must forgive foster parents when a move is unavoidable because the needs of the children are outside the foster parents' ability.

In circumstances when disruptions occur suddenly on the agency's end, foster parents have to forgive the agency too. This has happened to us in the past, as there have been instances when foster children have not ended up being placed into foster care after all, and the agency staff has forgotten to notify us. I have waited for hours before tracking down an after-hours case manager to ask them what was happening with the child and have heard apologies for forgetting to call to explain why the child was not coming to our home. Also, if an inappropriate placement selection later leads to a placement disruption, the agency staff should move a child without emotional retaliation toward the foster family. Foster parents should be kindly supported when these types of occurrences happen, and they want to grow from their experiences and be able to continue to try with another child when the next placement call comes in. Both foster families and agency staff need to stand up and say when they are wrong.

Lastly, foster-parent retention problems happen because of the ever-looming threat of an allegation. An allegation is a claim that something wrong has occurred in the foster home. Living through an allegation can shake a foster parent's resolve to stay with the vocation. Our set of five siblings, who lived with us for a year, never voiced a complaint about us or our home. They had hundreds of private meetings with social workers, teachers, therapists, doctors, and their own parents where they could have expressed any worry without us knowing. Unexpectedly though, as the county staff did exit interviews with the children after they left our home, there was a comment "of concern" the agency wanted to discuss with us. After weeks of secrecy and waiting, we found that the concern was that the preteen girl thought we liked her brothers more than her. We were genuinely sad to hear this because we certainly did not feel that way about her. We were probably most proud of her, in particular, and the successes she achieved in the time she lived with us. No allegations were substantiated (found to be true), but the vulnerability and heartache slices away at positive feelings of wanting to open up our hearts and our homes to others.

A key element in a foster parent's day-to-day support is absolutely going to come from peer foster friendships. This unwavering support is the primary reason, I think, foster parents can keep this journey going. Several families working closely together is how most of us realistically manage the daily demands of the children, our families, and the agency. Peer support gives us a safe place to vent with people who understand the hard work we do. We can bounce ideas off one another, and if all else fails, all of us will stop what we are doing to pick up an unruly child and keep them for a day or two just to let the other foster parent have time to reset. We have all needed this hurdle help at some point.

As an additional form of support, some agencies utilize emergency foster homes, which are an option for immediate short-term placement if an ideal match for a long-term foster home cannot be readily found. During this time, the children would be placed in a short-term or triage type of foster home. The goal of a short-term foster placement would be to allow the experienced foster parent time to assess the needs of the children from a caretaker's point of view and would also give the agency staff more time to identify potential family members for kinship placement or a well-suited long-term foster home. This type of intervention can decrease the need for removal later because a realistic evaluation of the child's needs is better understood before placing them in a regular foster home.

Another support measure in the retention of foster parents is our alternative caregiver network. These are individuals who have offered to get to know our family, go through the background-check process, agree to the agency discipline policy, and help support us in many ways. I could never put into words how much stamina foster caregiving takes, so having frequent rest times and knowing the children are in the fun, capable hands of our alternative caregivers is a huge factor in sustaining our stamina.

Several of these amazing alternative caregiving families have worked with us for many years and have learned the tricks of the trade of our foster children's antics. They understand that direct eyeball supervision of most foster children is best to promote the safest environment. They know to text and ask questions to confirm some of the stories they are being told. Overall, they have a knack for knowing what is permitted and what is not. Preteens Kathy and Miguel running off to play in the basement activity room together would not be permitted in our home, as they tried to tell a caregiver. Likewise, Jamal literally reported that he was allowed to swing down from the second story banister to the main floor, which clearly, he was not. We tell our foster children a special type of babysitter is watching them when we go out, and they know and uphold the foster-care rules.

Several of our alternative caregivers have gone above and beyond and have taken the routine care of our foster children to the next level by stocking needed items such as various sizes of underwear, sweatpants, T-shirts, and toothbrushes in their own homes in case our child has an unexpectant need. Once, on a business trip to Detroit, we received a call for a teen brother and sister who were sitting together in the agency waiting room, holding hands, and crying because they did not want to go to separate foster homes. The staff knew we were out of town but were finding it difficult to locate a home who could accept them both, so they called us anyway. We felt bad for the teens, because we always consider keeping siblings together so important, so we called an alternative caregiver friend and asked if she would take the children overnight until we came back into town the next day. Along with the emergency pajama set the agency provided, she pulled several items from her own stock to use because the children's clothes, hair, and bodies were so dirty. They wanted to throw their clothes and shoes away after they showered, and they were permitted. Our alternative caregivers make the difference, exceeding our expectations with their generosity, ingenuity, and kindness.

Foster parents burn out primarily because of situations centering around isolation, disruption, and allegations. We are frequently doing this job with a lack of adequate information. We wait through endless loops of referral hotlines hoping to get to a live voice when we have a situation brewing that needs instant assistance. Foster parents are not lightweights. We endure a lot; we keep going even when the going is tough. Mostly we love our work, but some changes would be welcomed.

Discussions that center around foster-care reform always address recruiting new foster families, but rarely is the retention aspect of already-established foster homes mentioned. Veteran foster parents, whom I consider anyone who withstands the system longer than two years, are valuable in their experience and knowledge. Plus, their training and home studies are already paid for! If foster families quit shortly after they get licensed, then money is lost. Having a more efficient system to place children in the best available homes initially means not having an inappropriate-leveled child placed for convenience. This would be better for the child and would reduce burnout of disenfranchised foster parents. Ultimately, boosting morale saves county dollars.

With thoughtful placements, emotional support from peers, and solid alternative caregivers, most placements will go well. Finding our niche and focusing on our individual strengths are the keys to better satisfaction to provide excellent care to the foster children with whom we have been entrusted.

CHAPTER 25: SOCIAL RESPONSIBILITY

Our life's work in raising our biological children, as well as our foster children, has centered around developing a sense of social responsibility in them. We think social responsibility is achieved first by helping a child heal and thrive and then by identifying and developing their natural abilities. Ideally the development of these abilities leads to a survival road map for their young lives. This process helps children become responsible for their own well-being and become strong enough to do their part, in return, for their community. We aim to raise social warriors who are not easily conquered by external pressures or vices.

Stabilization and building self-confidence start any child's journey to responsible adulthood. This seems especially true in the world of foster care because many children have never experienced solid support. Our top priority is to support everyone associated with the child's case plan, working towards eliminating the causes of the abuse or neglect. And, as foster parents, we work toward providing a home in which the child feels welcome, safe, and comfortable. As these beginning steps become more solidified, the healing and growing process can begin.

Omar came to us with many physical wounds that were a result of hard, blunt trauma. His arms and legs were full of bruises and scars in various stages of healing. Memories of severe beatings haunted his sleep. This sweet boy's story was heartbreaking, and we were wildly concerned about his safety. We spent months interacting with the caseworker to ensure that he was safe in every aspect of his life and that no further harm could come to him. His was a long and hard road learning to manage the giant stresses in his little life, but thanks to his heaven-sent adoptive parents, he is growing into an amazing young man who is kind, respectful, and has a heart of gold. Omar's maturing respect for himself has further evolved into respect for others. He uses his fantastic personality volunteering to help others through his church.

By acknowledging that we will not be able to heal our foster children completely during their time in foster care, we concentrate on what we as cheerleaders of children can get accomplished. Emphasis is always placed on stabilizing the children and making them feel worthy of healing from the adverse experiences of their past, helping them create new goals, and not being victims of their past forever. Ending victimization gives foster children a sense of normalcy.

Six-year-old Katie thought of herself as worthless and was fearful of everything. She was hesitant to talk or give her opinion on the most unimportant of matters. She threw her hands up and guarded herself when unexpected movements or sudden loud noises occurred nearby. We worked hard to build her will to survive one step at a time. We started with tending to her severe malnutrition and other immediate medical needs. Then we focused on helping her feel secure in our home and made sure to speak to her prior to moving suddenly to help calm her nervousness. Finally, we gingerly encouraged her to speak more and start giving her own opinions. Pulling her out of her shell was a slow process. As time passed, she was able to find craft hobbies that made her happy, and eventually she began to develop the ability to play.

Social lessons for Katie consisted of having her practice looking the teacher in the eye when she spoke and being more confident with her attempts to answer questions in class. Soon these small wins grew, and eventually she learned that the harder she worked, the "luckier" she got. In cooperation with her dedicated teachers, this timid child eagerly learned letters and sounds, which grew quickly into a love for reading and books. Her self-confidence grew as she earned special classroom jobs and started making friends. Eventually, we talked to her about having grit and not giving up at the first sign of difficulty. She learned through her own experiences that life might not be easy, but it is still good, and hard work pays off.

While the Internet has brought positives to our world, foster parents have their work cut out for them with all the negativity also passed along from the media. This is why many foster parents add tackling media influences to their list of things to accomplish during the time a foster child is entrusted to their care. We are faced with answering questions and trying to make sense of the happenings in the world today while also attempting to boost children socially and morally. It is a real challenge. Keeping explanations as simple as possible helps.

Bailey let mean comments she heard about herself online affect her morale. The persistent negativity made her think that the worst was always about to happen. Her mind couldn't let go of these messages, and she began losing sight of the goodness around her. Many of our evening talks centered around her choices of whether to spend time on schoolwork or on the negativity of social media. We tried to help her learn that her mental health and general well-being would improve if she ignored the cruelties that abounded on social media. While we can limit media exposure at home, it is always going to be available elsewhere, and she had to decide whether she was going to spend her life worrying about what others thought of her or whether she was going to work hard and be proud of the things she chose to accomplish, despite what others said.

When explaining polite society to our children, we remind them that being kind is more important than being right. One trick we like to teach is to say a comment in a positive way. They can use this tactic with friends, which helps decrease the chances of getting drawn into silly drama. For example, instead of agreeing that a peer's outfit looks dumb, they can pick one thing about the outfit they do like and limit their comment to something like: "I like her earrings the best." Or at a football practice when the older schoolboys are laughing at the peewee players' botched play, our foster son said, "Yeah, but look how hard that kid ran trying catch him." We teach that, on any level, judging is God's job. Ours is to respect ourselves and others. Clearly, judging a person does not really define who *they* are, but it definitely defines who *we* are. One day, Timmy asked me, "Why do some people get treated differently for doing the same thing wrong?" I told him that those people forgot to respect each other and made it okay to have different rules for different people. He said, "I just can't understand that." I know, dear, I know.

Treating others with mutual respect is a conscious decision of a responsible citizen. Kindness to one group of people and purposefully holding it back from another is discouraged. One foster teen, Hadley, asked me what racism was, and I asked her what she thought it meant. She said it meant being mean to someone for no reason. I asked, "You mean any person being mean to another person is racism?" She said, "No, only if their skin colors are different." So, restating, she and apparently her friends think being mean to someone who looks the same as you is just plain mean, but meanness between people with different skin tones is racism. I suggested to her the simpler practice of one person equals one person, no exceptions. Hadley said, "Ok, I guess that's easier to understand." Children believe what they see and hear. Wanting to treat others with respect is showing social maturity. The key word is wanting. Excluding one set of friends or one cultural group is both small-minded and immature.

Typically, almost all foster children have suffered some trauma tainting their social perception of authority figures. As adults, we have a responsibility to keep negative incidents that involve authority figures in perspective. Just like the horror stories heard about some foster parents and some foster children, negative perceptions about authority figures should not be the norm. We teach every child who has come through our home, as well as our biological children, how to respectfully interact with authorities, especially law enforcement, regardless of whether they are at Children's Services, in the courtroom, or on the street. Having hands in plain view and following all directions cooperatively and politely puts officials in the best position to make the decisions they must make, sometimes in a split second. We have taken training with simulators and know statistically that these safety guidelines help put the officials in the best position to exercise good judgment.

Most foster parents and authority figures are good and honest people trying to give the proper care to people in need. They do not do everything right; they are human after all. Unfortunately, we know parents who teach their children to fear all police officers and social workers and to run and hide if they see them. We can best serve our children by teaching them to be careful of the decisions they make today, which will affect all their tomorrows.

We demonstrate greeting every social worker, doctor, police officer, or court official in a friendly way and speaking to them respectfully. We take time to teach our children about how many of these people donate their time and talents to community activities they themselves benefit from, such as basketball clinics, mentoring programs, and bike giveaways. In the adult community, these same professionals support pregnancy centers, offer domestic violence recovery counseling, work with nursing home residents, and provide anonymous financial assistance to others. There are a thousand examples of socially responsible people who are dedicated to strengthening their communities. These selfless people are role models for children to learn to be other-centered through volunteerism.

One such lesson learned, through our town's Safety Town program, made a big impression on our foster son Noah. He knew if he saw a gun, he should recite the rhyme he learned, "Stop. Don't touch. Leave the area. Tell an adult." He used to run around the house chanting this warning all the time. When he came back into foster care the second time, he told us he used this the summer between his two stays at our house. Noah knew not to touch the gun he found at his dad's house, made his brother stay away from the gun, and told his grandmother about it. He may have saved a life that day.

Once stability and safety are secured for the foster child, we focus our time on developing a sense of social responsibility. The main part of social responsibility is educating our children in preparation for having a job as an adult. We look at the children's natural abilities, not necessarily their passion. We know some children will be advanced in academics, others in skilled or manual labor.

Sixteen-year-old Kemm had a passion for dancing and acting. Her natural abilities centered around her amazing memory. While we encouraged her fondness of drama as a hobby, we guided her toward a career in the business world where her sharp memory and strong work ethic serve her well. Every human has some talent that can be developed, and all people are worthy of feeling good about their level of achievement, whatever that level is. Nothing gets a child started on the road to being socially responsible like highlighting and evolving their abilities.

We field questions that come our way as children navigate and process the best ways to identify and build their abilities. One subject that we are sometimes broached about, from our older foster children, is their curiosity of jobs and why some people have more money than others. The ones who know about welfare benefits want to know why some people get it and why some people do not. One conversation on this topic started when our foster teen Ryan, thirteen, asked me, as our kitchen floor was being replaced, "How did you get your landlord to agree to a new floor?" I explained that we did not have a landlord and what home ownership meant. He was completely astounded because this was a situation that he had absolutely no familiarity with. Later at school, he was learning about personal finance, and Ryan correctly volunteered the difference between renting and owning a home. His teacher told me that he excelled in the financial discussions they had and was the first to complete a monthly budget project correctly. This conversation and others prompted talks about his career goals and dreams for the future.

Past foster teenager Candace called us out of the blue, probably ten years after she had left our home, to tell us that she remembered what it was like when she lived with us. Apparently "what we had" to her consisted of an intact family with an employed dad, a car that worked, groceries in our cupboard, and that beloved beach-themed bedroom she had decorated. She recalled how much we encouraged her drawing and drafting skills in school. She told us she had gotten her mental health issues under control, was attending counseling every week, and was currently employed with a computer company. She said she also had found a church to belong to that had a drug dependency support group. Candace—a teen I would have never betted on being touched by our family's mission—said she kept the vision of an intact family in her mind all these years as what she wanted to strive toward. That was one of those really neat days to be a foster parent!

Part of social responsibility is instilling a love of country to every generation we influence. My favorite sayings are from President Kennedy: "Ask not what your country can do for you, ask what you can do for your country," and Reverend Martin Luther King Jr.: "I have a dream that my four little children will one day live in a nation where they will not be judged by the color of their skin, but by the content of their character." Connecting each other with positive social experiences is what makes our communities and country thrive. My husband and I believe that the top parenting priorities should be to build self-confidence, foster a sense of respect toward self and others, develop a viable career path, and initiate beginner adult life skills to create children who are socially strong.

I would be remiss if I did not mention volunteering as it pertains to social responsibility. The benefits of doing a kind deed for someone else is the foundation of volunteerism. Children are capable of learning to volunteer early in life, which gives a sense of achievement to the child, maybe helps them learn a new skill, and gives them a rudimentary understanding of the meaning of empathy. All our children have had the chance to ring the bell for the Salvation Army Christmas kettle, work the annual school supply send off, march in the local parade, or volunteer at church. It is good for children to volunteer and witness other peoples' problems rather than just their own. Doing so helps them understand the world around them and see outside themselves. We stress that everyone can do some small, random act of kindness because there is always someone less fortunate in need.

Our downtown area is home to a bronze statue of a boy carrying a leaky boot. The story behind the statue is that the boy helped during the Civil War by taking water to the injured servicemen with the only thing he had—a boot with a hole. The boy plugged the hole with his hand and repeatedly carried lifesaving water to the injured soldiers.[14] We routinely tell this simple story to all the children who come through our home so they can learn the importance of helping others—even if it is just a drink of water from a leaky boot.

Lastly, there is a great deal of conversation about tolerance and diversity in the world today. Foster parents get to see diversity from all angles, which is one of the best parts of the job! We have had the privilege of taking in children from many ethnic backgrounds and have known and cared for children whose ancestry hails from Europe, Africa, Native America, Pacific Islands, Germany, Puerto Rico, Turkey, Finland, Somalia, Mexico, and Asia. We have suffered some tough moments when we met intolerant people, but our safety net is to "kill 'em with kindness." Cross-cultural fostering has brought us much joy, and we treasure the wonderfully unique friendships we have formed through the years. With every child who comes to our home, we get a new chance to keep learning. After all, people are far more alike than they are different. It is not so complicated. No one person is more loved by God than another; we are all created in His likeness.

Foster parenting is not like other professions; it is a behind-the-scenes commitment of the heart to give excellent care to someone else's child, build them up to succeed, and teach them the importance of their role in society. Foster parents need to understand an unwritten code of honor that most of us abide by: Be more kind and giving than is expected and love deeper than you think is possible. These are not guidelines found written in a handbook anywhere. When you get kicked in the gut, both figuratively and literally, offer up the suffering and keep working toward the goal of fostering love to one child at a time.

EPILOGUE

Not everyone wants to be a foster parent, but everyone can do something meaningful to help a foster child. Foster parents repeatedly hear, "I could never be a foster parent," which is completely understandable. However, please do not let that stop you from learning about the foster-care system and seeing if there is an avenue for your talent! All foster families need a vast amount of solid ongoing support. Extra help from the community is vital, and I can say without doubt that not once in our foster-care career did we take care of a child completely unassisted by others. Our extended family, friends, neighbors, and community members have been generous in their loyal support.

I have hundreds of stories that encompass the incredible hurdle help we have received from our community. Thankfully, many generous people are interested in foster care, which no doubt benefits our foster children. A wise teacher from our parish school once said, "If your cup of blessing is overflowing, and you are generous with giving your blessings away, God will have a reason to bestow more blessings upon you." We are reminded to share our cup of blessings, and we know that more will come. Without fail, we have witnessed this time and time again.

One day at the pediatrician's office, a nurse yelled out to all the parents in the waiting room, "Whose baby this be?" After a moment of dread wondering which mom was going to claim the child (who apparently must have been doing something wrong), I looked up, and of course the child was mine. I reluctantly stood, as the other moms chuckled, and told her Aisha was with me. The kind lady smiled and said to come back to the exam room so she could show me how to treat her scalp condition and style her unruly hair. Now, in my defense, I had only had Aisha for a day, and she had a lot of hair, but I dutifully obeyed. This lady was sweet and kind with her instructions about combing out the hair correctly, preventing a worse condition called tender scalp. She assured me we did not want that. She demonstrated with great expertise the use of several hair products and how to carefully work through her matted hair. That was my first of many hair lessons, but I'll never forget that funny day with the nurse who cared enough to help.

Other community members who have found unique ways to support our foster-care vocation are the ladies in our community who scour garage sales and bring their finds of books, clothes, shoes, and toys over from time to time. They clean the items and drop the discovered treasures off on our front porch, all as a charitable hobby. One day they discovered a true prize—a retiring teacher's garage sale which was perfect timing prior to the COVID-19 shutdowns. This provided us with wonderful materials for teaching foster children lessons at home.

One parishioner drove my foster son Tre to preschool a couple of days a week after she left the daily 8am Mass. She said she did not mind because the timing worked, and she was already out and about for the day. Because of her generosity, I did not have to wake his little sister Gabby quite so early in the morning, all winter long. Another church friend not only donated beautiful bunk beds to us, but her family came over and assembled the structure too. I cannot express how much these good deeds conserved our energy that year with eight foster children in the house.

Several thoughtful families donate beautiful clothes to us from their own children. We keep the articles of clothing that we need and then divide up the extra items to share with other families with foster children. Some of the families we share with have five boys, another has six boys (and three girls), and another has six girls! We also have friends who save their used electronics and donate them to us for our older foster children to have. The foster children love feeling like they fit in with their peers with these occasional luxuries.

A neighboring community church group has gotten several of their ladies auxiliary members certified as official alternative caregivers. They take requests for short babysitting sessions and cook a meal when needed. The husbands and young adult children in the group have helped with providing handyman repairs when needed. A theme park proprietor heard of our family and donated swim passes for our foster children to come and enjoy their facilities for a whole summer, free of charge.

Charitable acts of kindness come in all forms. People have provided ice cream dates, swimming afternoons, miniature-golf excursions, trips to the zoo, and even an adventure to an amusement park. Our neighbors have helped us to buy bikes and helmets for many of our children. A doctor's office staff donates Christmas gifts each year. A friend's business has taken a special interest in our foster children and helps us with special occasion gifts. One family we know has a big country lot and has had our family over to play with their farm animals and allows the kids to romp around in their huge yard. Mud is always involved. Several children have had the great thrill of catching their first fish at their lake. Talk about a priceless gift! The children interact with another deeply caring family, and they get to experience many new sounds, feelings, smells, and activities on a farm! What a delightful opportunity for our children to get to hold a colorful chicken or feed the baby ducks. This day always makes it into their Lifebook memory albums!

My own father's superpower is to adapt toys and equipment for handicapped children. He has an ingenious engineering mind and a charitable heart, and he always finds a clever way to create the exact apparatus I seem to need for a child's special needs. He has designed equipment with adaptations for riding toys, stability supports for the rocking horse, and handrails for baby equipment. His special abilities add immeasurable quality of life and maximum entertainment to children with both physical and mental impairments. My uncle uses his love of gardening to stock the local food bank with fresh produce throughout the growing season each year. These people are all selfless and kind examples of God's love.

Ron and I joke that we are happily starting to collect a lot of children. If the foster child's family agrees, we try to see "old fosters" at least once a year. We typically take a present with us because we want the children to know we remember them and that they are important to us. Promoting self-esteem and bonding is the continued goal of foster parents long after the children return home. The help and support from our community members are what allow us to care for foster children years after they leave us.

Professionals have the unique opportunity to support foster children as well. If you are a pastor or a minister, please help facilitate interest in child welfare. Sometimes you have unique knowledge of a family who has an interest in fostering or adopting. You may also be aware of families who have extra time or talents to share. If the occasion arises, consider helping them to meet up and connect with a foster family. I would estimate that five strong helper families are needed to support one foster home. Consistent, reliable support is what foster parents need from our communities. Lastly, encourage your congregations to pray for the youth of our country and for significant improvements in the war on drugs and human trafficking. The lifelong effects on children are devastating.

If you are a business owner, please consider assisting foster homes in any way you are able. We received a boy, Maks, at

10pm one night who happily informed us that his birthday was "tomorrow." We woke up early to run to our local bakery and asked them if they could grab a stocked cake and write "Happy 5th Birthday, Maks" on it. While they were working to box it up, I told them about the whirlwind ten hours we had getting his birthday celebration together. I pulled out my wallet to pay for the cake, and the ladies thanked me for my service to foster care and told me the cake would be on them that day. I drove all the way home with tears in my eyes.

One year, at our foster-parent appreciation banquet, our donated thank-you gift was Keno cards (still not sure what those are) and poker chips. Some of us were appalled, and some of us laughed wondering if this gesture was maybe meant to be a joke. What we need more urgently are disinfecting wipes, laundry detergent, and batteries. I got a surprise years later when I told this story to an associate helping me shop for a washing machine. She and her manager nonchalantly chatted with me on my way out of the store, by way of the laundry detergent aisle, and asked me to take a large container of laundry soap home to go with the new washing machine. That unexpected surprise made me cry too!

If you own a business that teaches ballet, sports skills, or gymnastics, please consider discount pricing for foster families. The cost of foster caregiving is difficult to compare state by state since the cost of living differs, but also because what foster parents are expected to cover for the child is inconsistent. However, the national average of raising a child is roughly $36/day,[15] and foster parents are receiving reimbursement for care of a foster child at roughly $18-25/day.[16] This leaves approximately $300-500/month per foster child to be incurred by the foster family. There are not always excessive dollars left over for these meaningful extras that we want all children to experience.

If your interest in foster care goes further than how the nuts and bolts of the program run, consider offering to be a mentor to a foster child in a family you know. Foster homes are filled with needy children yearning to have people come forward and offer to help. Children love to learn to play piano, sew, and play Checkers. Adults who pass along stories, traditions, and knowledge to the younger generation are also sharing invaluable life lessons. My father helped Sergeant repair, sand, stain, and rehang the oak door he damaged one day at our home. It would have taken less time and effort for Dad to do the repair himself, but the grandfatherly time spent teaching the mischievous preteen a skill of precision and patience was the bigger gift.

Our society needs more people to become familiar and comfortable with foster children and the foster-care system. It does take a village to raise a child. Volunteerism has long been known as an effective treatment for feelings of loneliness or sadness that empty nesters and retirees can have. Lots of people still have room in their hearts and homes for some child interaction time. The appropriate foster child could become a big blessing to an elder and the elder a friend to the foster child. This is God's work, and it is such a blessing when we make time for these children placed in the foster-care system through no fault of their own.

Being good stewards of God's children can come in many forms. If your heart is open to becoming a foster and/or adoptive parent, follow the calling and do it with your whole heart. On the day I was telling my dear high school pal that I was thinking about getting back into foster care again, she looked at me like I was foolishly overthinking the whole idea. Her response to me was, "Just do it!" Ha, easy for her to say. Actually though, she was right. I called the agency the next day. Sometimes, you just need to take that leap of faith. Thanks, Jackie. We have never regretted our decision to foster.

There are endless possibilities associated with helping others. Every positive adult interaction a child experiences helps alter the story of their past and move them toward a stronger future. If you are a person of influence in your community and this book finds its way into your busy life, thank you for taking the time to read about this important issue affecting every state in our country. Please consider what foster parents and foster children are being asked to endure daily. Every hour of every day of every year, foster families take in children with all kinds of needs and behaviors, both known and unknown. The foster children are welcomed into our homes with no strings attached.

Many blessings have come to our family because of these special and resilient children. We have gotten to know more dear friends and colleagues than we would have met otherwise. The kindhearted staff members at CSB and peer foster families are like an extended family. The knowledge, experience, time, and comradery that those involved in foster care are willing to share with each other is immeasurable. These friendships make the tough days worthwhile!

With her fists poised on her little four-year-old hips, and a pout on her face, foster daughter Andie adamantly told me that she was not going home because "I like foster place!" Surprisingly, her eleven-year-old brother peered from around the corner and said "Yeah, I don't want to go either. I liked having a mom."

People talk about being called to a vocation their entire lives, and I am blessed that mine has been to be a mother and a foster mother.

Foster care never stops pulling at your heartstrings, but the job is still the best, and I would not trade it for the world. We are honored to have parented these amazing human beings. They are funny, silly, and mischievous, but mostly they are gifts from God!

"Since we have gifts that differ according to the grace given to us, let us exercise them: if prophecy, in proportion to the faith; if ministry, in ministering; if one is a teacher, in teaching; if one exhorts, in exhortation; if one contributes, in generosity; if one is over others, with diligence; if one does acts of mercy, with cheerfulness." - Romans 12:6-8 (RSV)

NOTES

1. Bill Oser, National Orphan Train Complex Museum and Research Center, Accessed September 25, 2021, orphantraindepot.org/history/orphan-train-rider-stories/bill-oser.

2. Lisa Wingate. *Before We Were Yours*. Ballantine Books, 2017.

3. Irene Clements, "We Have to Stop Losing Half of Foster Parents in the First Year," The Imprint, May 18, 2018, imprintnews.org/opinion/stop-losing-half-foster-parents-first-year/30904.

4. Mary Boo, "Number of Adoptions Highest Ever; Foster Care Population Down," North American Council on Adoptable Children, Accessed February 11, 2022, nacac.org/2020/01/10/number-of-adoptions-highest-ever-foster-care-population-down.

5. Emily Kernan, "Keeping Siblings Together: Past, Present, and Future," National Center for Youth Law, Accessed September 25, 2021, youthlaw.org/publication/keeping-siblings-together-past-present-and-future.

6. Chapter 5101:2-7, "Foster Care," Ohio Laws and Administrative Rules, Legislative Service Commission, Accessed September 25, 2021, codes.ohio.gov/ohio-administrative-code/chapter-5101:2-7.

7. Emily Kernan, "Keeping Siblings Together: Past, Present, and Future," National Center for Youth Law, Accessed September 25, 2021, youthlaw.org/publication/keeping-siblings-together-past-present-and-future.

8. "Mother Teresa," Biography.com, A&E Television Networks, April 27, 2017, biography.com/religious-figure/mother-teresa.

9. Heather Featherston, "Contact with Birth Parents after Adoption," Lifetime Adoption, September 16, 2020, lifetimeadoption.com/adoptivefamilies-contact-with-birth-parents-after-adoption.

10. Foster Cline and Jim Fay. *Parenting with Love and Logic: Teaching Children Responsibility*. Colorado Springs: NavPress, 2020.

11. "Understanding the Effects of Maltreatment on Brain Development," Child Welfare Information Gateway, Issue

Brief (2015), childwelfare.gov/pubs/issue-briefs/brain-development.

12. Chapter 2151.353: "Orders of Disposition of Abused, Neglected or Dependent Child," Ohio Laws and Administrative Rules, Legislative Service Commission, Accessed September 25, 2021, codes.ohio.gov/ohio-revised-code/section-2151.353.

13. "The Importance of a Father in a Child's Life," Pediatric Associates of Franklin, Accessed February 11, 2022, pediatricsoffranklin.com/resources-and-education/pediatric-care/the-importance-of-a-father-in-a-childs-life.

14. "Boy and the Boot," RoadsideAmerica.com, Accessed November 15, 2021, roadsideamerica.com/story/43194.

15. Elyssa Kirkham, "A Breakdown of the Cost of Raising a Child," Plutus Foundation, February 2, 2021, plutusfoundation.org/2021/a-breakdown-of-the-cost-of-raising-a-child.

16. Sarah East, "Financial Guide to Being a Foster Parent," MoneyGeek.com, June 23, 2021, moneygeek.com/financial-planning/managing-finances-as-a-foster-parent.

BIBLIOGRAPHY

Annie E. Casey Foundation, "Top Causes of Staff Turnover at Child Welfare Agencies—And What to Do About It," March 4, 2019, aecf.org/blog/top-causes-of-staff-turnover-at-child-welfare-agencies-and-what-to-do-about.

Anxiety and Depression Association of America, "Symptoms of PTSD," Accessed February 11, 2022, adaa.org/understanding-anxiety/posttraumatic-stress-disorder-ptsd/symptoms.

Biography.com, "Mother Teresa," A&E Television Networks, April 27, 2017, biography.com/religious-figure/mother-teresa.

Boo, Mary, "Number of Adoptions Highest Ever; Foster Care Population Down," North American Council on Adoptable Children, Accessed February 11, 2022, nacac.org/2020/01/10/number-of-adoptions-highest-ever-foster-care-population-down.

"Boy and the Boot," RoadsideAmerica.com, Accessed November 15, 2021, roadsideamerica.com/story/43194.

Chapter 2151.353: "Orders of Disposition of Abused, Neglected or Dependent Child," Ohio Laws and Administrative Rules, Legislative Service Commission, Accessed September 25, 2021, codes.ohio.gov/ohio-revised-code/section-2151.353.

Chapter 5101:2-7, "Foster Care," Ohio Laws and Administrative Rules, Legislative Service Commission, Accessed September 25, 2021, codes.ohio.gov/ohio-administrative-code/chapter-5101:2-7.

Child Welfare Information Gateway, "Understanding the Effects of Maltreatment on Brain Development," Issue Brief (2015), childwelfare.gov/pubs/issue-briefs/brain-development.

Child Welfare Information Gateway, US Department of Health and Human Services, Accessed September 25, 2021, childwelfare.gov.

Clements, Irene, "We Have to Stop Losing Half of Foster Parents in the First Year," The Imprint, May 18, 2018, imprintnews.org/opinion/stop-losing-half-foster-parents-first-year/30904.

Cline, Foster, and Jim Fay. *Parenting with Love and Logic: Teaching Children Responsibility*. Colorado Springs: NavPress, 2020.

East, Sarah, "Financial Guide to Being a Foster Parent," MoneyGeek.com, June 23, 2021, moneygeek.com/financial-planning/managing-finances-as-a-foster-parent.

Featherston, Heather, "Contact with Birth Parents after Adoption," Lifetime Adoption, September 16, 2020, lifetimeadoption.com/adoptivefamilies-contact-with-birth-parents-after-adoption.

Ignatius Catholic Bible: Revised Standard Version. Ignatius Press: 2005.

Kaplan Early Learning Company, "Understanding the Six Types of Neglect," Accessed September 25, 2021, kaplanco.com/ii/six-types-of-neglect.

Kernan, Emily, "Keeping Siblings Together: Past, Present, and Future," National Center for Youth Law, Accessed September 25, 2021, youthlaw.org/publication/keeping-siblings-together-past-present-and-future.

Kirkham, Elyssa, "A Breakdown of the Cost of Raising a Child," Plutus Foundation, February 2, 2021, plutusfoundation.org/2021/a-breakdown-of-the-cost-of-raising-a-child.

Li, Pamela, MS, MBA, "Early Brain Development in Children," Parenting for Brain, Updated January 31, 2022, parentingforbrain.com/brain-development.

National Responsible Fatherhood Clearinghouse, "Father Involvement in Education," Accessed September 25, 2021, fatherhood.gov/for-dads/father-involvement-education.

Oser, Bill, National Orphan Train Complex Museum and Research Center, Accessed September 25, 2021, orphantraindepot.org/history/orphan-train-rider-stories/bill-oser.

Pediatric Associates of Franklin, "The Importance of a Father in a Child's Life," Accessed February 11, 2022, pediatricsoffranklin.com/resources-and-education/pediatric-care/the-importance-of-a-father-in-a-childs-life.

Reach Out and Read, "A Daily Experience, a Lifelong Benefit," Accessed February 11, 2022, reachoutandread.org/our-story/importance-of-reading-aloud.

Rementería, JoséLuis, MD, S. Janakammal, MD, and Melvin Hollander, MD. "Multiple Births in Drug-Addicted Women," *American Journal of Obstetrics and Gynecology* 122, no. 8 (1975): p. 958-960. ajog.org/article/0002-9378(75)90355-5/fulltext.

The Understood Team, "Understanding Sensory Processing Issues," Understood for All, Inc., Accessed November 15, 2021, understood.org/articles/en/understanding-sensory-processing-issues.

Wingate, Lisa. *Before We Were Yours*. Ballantine Books, 2017.

ABOUT THE AUTHOR

Kathleen and her husband Ron reside in Wadsworth, Ohio. They love spending time with their adult children and participating in the exciting events happening in their young lives. To date, Kathleen and Ron have fostered 135 foster children. Kathleen's favorite moments happen around her gardening no matter if she is teaching children about planting or watching strawberry juice trickle down their smiling faces. She also enjoys woodworking with her dad. While Kathleen and Ron's main focus is fostering, they also enjoy advocating for children in the foster-care system through speaking engagements. Find out more about Kathleen and her family at KathleenPaydo.com.

CPSIA information can be obtained
at www.ICGtesting.com
Printed in the USA
LVHW092218041022
729963LV00005B/319